WINNING

WITH

STOCKS

WINNING
WITH
STOCKS

The Smart Way to
Pick Investments, Manage Your Portfolio,
and Maximize Profits

MICHAEL C. THOMSETT

AMACOM

American Management Association

New York • Atlanta • Brussels • Chicago • Mexico City • San Francisco
Shanghai • Tokyo • Toronto • Washington, D.C.

This publication is designed to provide accurate and authoritative information in regard to the subject matter covered. It is sold with the understanding that the publisher is not engaged in rendering legal, accounting, or other professional service. If legal advice or other expert assistance is required, the services of a competent professional person should be sought.

Library of Congress Cataloging-in-Publication Data

Thomsett, Michael C.
    Winning with stocks : the smart way to pick investments, manage your portfolio, and maximize profits / Michael C. Thomsett.
        p. cm.
    Includes index.
    ISBN-13: 978-0-8144-0986-2
    ISBN-10: 0-8144-0986-5
    1. Investments.   2. Stocks.   3. Speculation.   I. Title.

HG6041.T46 2008
332.63'22—dc22

2008017989

Printing number

10   9   8   7   6   5   4   3   2   1

CONTENTS

PREFACE

Creating Your Comprehensive Program

The market. The idea of people trading money in and out of stocks, whether $100 or $10 billion, is exciting. It represents the epitome of the free market and of capitalism. While many people criticize the free economy, it has become truly global in recent years, and the movement and exchange of capital fuels the world's economy. It always has and it always will. But the changes brought about by improved information technology, the Internet, and the opening of many borders since the end of the Cold War have all expanded *the market* so that today it is easy for anyone to invest virtually anywhere—instantly.

This miracle brings with it many new risks. While in the past information was expensive, difficult to find, and untimely, today there is too much information. The modern challenge is deciding which information is useful, and which is not. This book concentrates on specific investment tools that help you to develop the means to control your individual portfolio, research, and decision-making process. These tools work together in forming your program for creating and managing profits. Advice in the financial press is either too broad and general, focuses on one small part of the total picture, or distorts and exaggerates the importance of market developments. This book puts together a program for the informed study of stocks, to improve your overall performance in an ever-changing market environment.

The stock market in the United States is the most popular investment market in the world, used not only by millions of individuals, but also by institutional investors: mutual funds, pension plans, insurance companies. Just about everyone who invests, has a retirement plan, or works for a large company is *in* the market. But how much do they really know about picking stocks? That is the big question answered by ***Winning with Stocks***.

An irony of how people invest is that—especially in the stock market—rumor, gossip, and opinion are given greater weight than research. This is a widespread flaw, with "the crowd" more often wrong than right (giving rise to contrarian strategies), and with the market characterized more by emotion than by logic. It has been said that if the market were a person, he or she would probably be in therapy.

Stocks can be selected by sector, reputation, or price. Some people like the fundamentals (financial information), others prefer technical analysis (charting patterns, price trends, and volume/price study). Both fundamental and technical schools offer valuable ideas.

In ***Winning with Stocks***, the reader is going to find a short list of the most valuable indicators (fundamental and technical) for picking stocks. On the fundamental side are ratios designed to quantify financial and working capital strength (current ratio, debt ratio) and profitability (revenue trend, net return). Technical indicators include price history, trading volatility, and trading range trends. Combination indicators include dividend yield, earnings per share, and the all-important price/earnings (P/E) ratio. The author provides suggestions about picking stocks using these limited number of tests.

This book is aimed at the novice or investor/trader with limited experience. The intention of this book is to explain the market in a spectrum of risks and opportunities, so that the reader will be able to make an informed decision about how to make profits while limiting risks in the stock market.

WINNING

WITH

STOCKS

A SHORT HISTORY OF
THE STOCK MARKET

The stock market is a fascinating cultural and financial place with a rich history. Before the telephone, communication was virtually impossible beyond the walls of the exchange or, in the case of the American Stock Exchange (AMEX), out on the street, because the exchange could not afford a building, thus its nickname, "the curb." In those days, the Philadelphia Stock Exchange (PHX) was at great disadvantage because traders in New York knew days ahead of others what goods were arriving by ship. So the PHX set up a series of men on hills with mirrors and telescopes, and messages were conveyed from New York to Philadelphia in less than one hour.

Because trading in the old days was limited to the exchange, only brokers and dealers were able to trade; the market simply was not available to the average person, an idea that is unthinkable today. Major advances included the telegraph, ticker tape, telephone, and of course, the computer. All of these changes have vastly improved the ability of people to communicate and to trade. This chapter introduces you to many of the most common errors investors make; by knowing these you are better equipped to avoid falling into the common market traps. This is followed by a brief history of the market itself, which is not only fascinating and interesting, but also demonstrates how we arrived at the system we have today.

The modern market is cheap, efficient, and well regulated. Today, more than ever before, the market has become truly democratic. Anyone with a few hundred dollars can buy shares of any listed company through a free online brokerage account, pay little or nothing for opening that account, and trade for only a few dollars. You no longer need to rely on expensive stockbrokers offering advice you really don't need. You can find your own research through books, the Internet, investment clubs, and association membership. In today's market, anyone willing to research for themselves and to study the market has a better chance than ever before to create and manage a stock portfolio.

Even so, *caveat emptor* continues to apply in the stock market as it does elsewhere. You cannot trust other people to make decisions for you, tell you where to invest, or ensure profitability. One reason for studying the long history of the market is to come to an understanding of the many problems inherent in any venue where a lot of money changes hands. Greed dominates the market, and that fact is unavoidable. The market attracts not only millions of honest, hardworking people who want to build security for themselves and their families, but also a variety of con artists and outright thieves. Unfortunately, many of these "market lowlifes" exist and thrive among all of us and often function as advisers, financial planners, analysts, stockbrokers, and online marketing companies offering "free" advice on how to get rich—they are everywhere.

The experience most people are going to have in the market will be largely positive, based not on any assurance of safety by government regulators, but by the simple fact that everyone is in control of their own destiny. This includes your portfolio. If you are realistic, willing to work and learn how the market functions, and you understand that profit potential always comes with risk, there is nothing to prevent you from enjoying the amazing "freedom to invest and profit" that you can have in the U.S. stock market.

A Starting Point: Avoiding the Mistakes of the Past

A history usually begins at the oldest point and moves forward. Before going back in time, however, it makes sense to begin at the end to expose the most common errors people make when they invest in the stock market. Knowing the history of the market is valuable and important, but even before you read about that, it is equally important to know what mistakes other people often make. History repeats itself. Everyone has heard this before, and it makes sense to know that most people are prone to fall into the same traps as those who have gone before. Thus, studying common errors is valuable intelligence, because it helps you to avoid those same problems.

One cynical point of view about this was expressed by George Bernard Shaw, who mused, "If history repeats itself, and the unexpected always happens, how incapable must Man be of learning from experience." This point of view is actually quite common in the market, but it is fatalistic and assumes that no one can overcome the errors of the past. If this is true, then you might as well turn over your money to a mutual fund and hope that its management is better than average. Contrary to that cynical point of view, it is possible for hardworking people to make informed decisions and to beat market averages, simply by observing (a) what others have done to lose money, (b) the mistakes that recur in the market, and (c) how specific indicators do, in fact, lead you to profits consistently.

Among the mistakes investors make are eight of the most important, listed below and also summarized in Table 1-1.

Mistake #1: Investing with More Risk Than You Can Afford

Risk—the chance that you will lose rather than gain—is an inherent attribute in all investments; there are no risk-free investments. A fully insured, guaranteed savings account contains the risk that income will not beat the combination of inflation and taxes, so even that represents a specific risk.

In the stock market, risk usually refers to *market risk*, or the risk

TABLE 1-1. EIGHT COMMON INVESTOR MISTAKES

Mistake #1: Investing with more risk than you can afford

Mistake #2: Chasing income but forgetting cash flow

Mistake #3: Limiting your investing horizon

Mistake #4: Overlooking the essential research

Mistake #5: Buying and selling at the wrong time

Mistake #6: Assuming the entry price is the starting point

Mistake #7: Believing higher-priced stocks are always expensive

Mistake #8: Worrying too much and being impatient

associated specifically with the price per share of stock. If you buy 100 shares at $50 per share and pay $5,000 and the stock's market value then falls to $45, you lose $500. A worthwhile exercise is to begin by defining your *risk tolerance,* or your ability to take risks and to afford possible losses. Stock risk is often spotted by way of volatility, the tendency for prices to move around. High-volatility stocks are often erratic and have a broad trading range, and low-volatility stocks tend to trade within a narrower price range.

Once you have identified what you can afford in terms of risk, it is easier to match your risk tolerance to companies whose stock histories are a good fit. Many people—including those who define their risk tolerance in advance—invest in inappropriate ways, taking risks they cannot afford. This is perhaps the most common mistake investors make. For example, many investors define themselves as conservative and "in it for the long term," and then trade like speculators.

MISTAKE #2: CHASING INCOME BUT FORGETTING CASH FLOW

The emphasis of income in the market is easy to understand. Everyone wants to buy bargain-priced stocks and cash in on a big price run-up. To a lesser degree, dividends are also a form of income but the dividend rate is at times overlooked. Investors tend to focus exclusively on profit potential but overlook the equally impor-tant cash flow, or the availability of cash when you need it.

For example, if you invest in stock that does not go up in value, you might determine that you need to keep your money tied up for several months. This might be especially true in cyclical stocks, whose economic cycle is tied to the calendar or to the economy. However, if it turns out that you need those funds before the cycle goes into an uptrend, you have to sell shares at a loss. This cash flow risk means that you cannot afford to hold onto positions as long as necessary to create profits. Because you have to take out funds for other purposes, the timing is poor for some of those long-term investments.

MISTAKE #3: LIMITING YOUR INVESTING HORIZON

It is easy to become myopic in the stock market. Once you find something that works, the tendency is to stick with it. For example, if you buy shares of an energy company and make a profit, you might believe that this sector is a "sure thing." But if your timing is poor, that does not necessarily apply. This is why most people sug-gest that you diversify your investment capital among several differ-ent stocks, sectors, and markets.

These different markets may include non-stock areas like bond mutual funds, real estate, options and futures, or precious metals. You can also diversify by buying shares of equity mutual funds or exchange-traded funds (ETFs). Effective diversification protects you from a broad overall loss due to a failure in a single company or sector. Those whose investing horizon is limited tend to be close-minded to the concept of diversification, so they are at greater risk. As long as investment capital remains in too few stocks or markets, the risk remains. The more capital focused in singular stocks or sectors, the greater the risk.

MISTAKE #4: OVERLOOKING THE ESSENTIAL RESEARCH

There are actually four distinct schools of thought about stock market research. First, those who believe in *fundamental analysis* rely on the financial reports issued by companies and their auditors or reports filed with the Securities and Exchange Commission (SEC), which regulates publicly traded corporations. A fundamental investor reads the balance sheet and income statement as well as narrative sections of reports and then develops a series of useful ratio tests to compare companies and to follow trends that appear within the company itself.

The second school of thought is *technical analysis*, which focuses on price movement of a stock and chart patterns. Technical analysts believe that specific chart patterns and short-term trends anticipate future price movement, and that the shape of the trading range itself (the distance between high and low prices over a period of time) defines volatility (safety) and anticipates near-term price movement.

The third is a combination, and this is the most sensible approach. By using aspects of both fundamental and technical analysis, information is gathered from different sources and based on a different series of assumptions, you make informed decisions.

Fourth is the largest group of all, containing investors who buy and sell stock with no valid information whatsoever. They watch price movement, go on investment chat lines and exchange information or simply read what others have written, and make decisions impulsively, often with very flawed information. For example, in 2007, a comment on a Yahoo! (YHOO) message board about one of the national home builders predicted that the stock would plummet and the company would go broke, specifically because with increased foreclosures, the company had to compete for a limited market. In other words, home buyers would choose foreclosed homes rather than buying a new home from the builder. This is insane. There are really only a small number of foreclosed properties at any given time, and the market for purchasing foreclosed homes is vastly different from the market for newly constructed properties. Even so, this is typical of the nonsense that can be found on Internet message boards—illogical, emotional, and at times self-serving (for example, if someone buys stock and the price falls, they may perform a *pump and dump*, going online and talking up the stock hoping others will buy shares, a practice that is illegal).

The point about comparing schools of investigation is this: You should plan to gain insight from whatever valuable source you can find, including both fundamental and technical analysis. But when it comes to opinions of people you do not know, unsolicited advice, or rumor and gossip, you will do well to avoid making any decisions based on those sources. They are the most common and the least reliable.

MISTAKE #5: BUYING AND SELLING AT THE WRONG TIME

The most famous maxim about investing is "Buy low and sell high." As trite as this might sound, it is important to remember because many people do exactly the opposite. It is useful to realize how most people view what goes on in short-term price trends. They assume, quite often, that whatever has happened most recently is going to continue happening in the future. Of course, this is illogical, but the market is ruled by two primary emotions: greed and fear. In fact, you will be wise to replace "Buy low and sell high" with a different maxim: "Bulls and bears can both make money, but the market is ruled by pigs and chickens."

On the greed side, as prices rise it is easy to believe that the trend will keep going in the same direction. Anyone owning stock holds onto it expecting further price growth and, in fact, they refuse to sell and miss out on *more* profit. So the prudent idea of taking profits—even when the value has doubled—is more often ignored than followed. An investor who does not already own stock will respond to price run-ups by buying shares, hoping to get in on the bonanza. This works sometimes, but it is also interesting to observe that buying activity in a stock is often at its greatest at the moment that prices peak and a downtrend begins.

On the fear side, as prices fall it is just as easy to believe that the whole market is going to crash. In this mode, investors are likely to sell when prices fall, hoping to avoid further declines. That is prudent in some cases, but most of the time a steep decline actually is an opportunity to buy shares at a cheap price. When fear dominates an investor's mind, it is impossible to think clearly.

When greed and fear dominate, people tend to buy high and sell low—the exact opposite of what they should be doing. For the astute, calm investor who is able to step back from these common emotional gut reactions, recognizing the timing opportunities of price run-up and steep decline are great opportunities in the market.

Mistake #6: Assuming the Entry Price Is the Starting Point

This mistake is worth keeping in mind, because it is so common. Stock prices are constantly rising and falling as buyers and sellers vie for control and exchange the momentum with one another. Prices rise and investors sell to take profits, which weakens demand and drives prices down; then investors buy at a bargain price, increasing demand and forcing prices up. There are dozens of possible influences on stock prices, and they are continually moving back and forth in response.

The common assumption among investors is to treat their purchase price per share as a starting point, when in fact it is simply the latest entry in the price continuum. For example, someone buys stock at $50 per share and immediately their assumption is that the stock is going to move upward. When it moves down instead or, more typically, floats up and down to prices on both sides of $50 per share, the investor is disappointed. The stock was supposed to rise, not fall or float.

This brings up an important concept: In the stock market, timing counts. Short- and long-term price momentum define how and why price trends come and go as they do. So if you happen to buy shares at the top of a price momentum swing, you are probably going to pay too much; and if you happen to buy at the bottom of a momentum swing, you will time your purchase well, at least until the momentum swings back in the other direction.

Mistake #7: Believing Higher-Priced Stocks Are Always Expensive

The math of the stock market is often confusing and easy to misread. A popular belief is that a $25 stock is worth half as much as a $50 stock. This is a misleading assumption. The price per share is not the definitive valuation point. For example, a company with 20 million shares at $25 per share is worth exactly the same as one with 10 million shares at $50 per share. In order to determine a company's "value" or whether its stock is a bargain, you need to look at other criteria, such as the price-to-earnings ratio (P/E ratio), which is also called the multiple. The price of a share of stock is divided by earnings per share, and the answer tells you how many times earnings the stock is trading. A low P/E implies the stock is cheap, and as the P/E gets quite high, it becomes a higher-risk investment. A stock trading between a P/E of 8 and 20 is reasonably priced, for example, compared to a stock with a P/E of 65.

The math problems of the market are not limited to misperceptions about the meaning of the price per share. The way that daily changes are reported can be misleading as well. For example, the financial news programs like to report the daily price change in the number of points. So two stocks, each rising by four points, have had a very good day. But they are not necessarily the same. For example, a stock selling at $20 per share rising four points has grown by 20 percent, which is very impressive. But another stock, selling at $200 per share, has only risen 2 percent on the same day. Although the reporting might be the same—both stocks rose four points—the $20 stock had 10 times *more* movement in value because its share price is lower.

MISTAKE #8: WORRYING TOO MUCH AND BEING IMPATIENT

An old saying tells us that "the market climbs a wall of worry." This refers to investor attitudes about all markets, including those whose prices are rising. Yes, they are rising today, but what about tomorrow? Experienced investors understand that when you get so overconfident that you stop worrying, you have set yourself up for a fall. Smart investors worry continually. As markets move down, they worry about more downward movement. As markets move up, they worry about a reversal.

The solution is patience. Inexperienced investors can easily get hooked on the action of the market, wanting to make a decision every day, take profits, and expose themselves to ever greater opportunities. But in the market, change does not always occur every day for every stock. An experienced investor knows that, as yet another old saying goes, "the market rewards patience." This is practiced in many forms, including waiting out short-term price movement (a speculative point of view) to holding stock over many years (a more conservative "value investing" point of view agreeing with people like Warren Buffett).

Your individual history as an investor is going to depend on how well you observe these common mistakes and avoid repeating them. But in addition to every person's individual history, the overall market is an interesting, colorful, and varied place where commerce has taken place for hundreds of years. Every investor will appreciate a brief overview of the stock market's history to demonstrate how it has arrived where it is today. However, in addition to watching out for the common mistakes other investors have made, it is equally important to ask the right questions before proceeding with any investment plan.

Your Most Important Questions

If people are doomed to repeat the past, then there is no point in trying to anticipate the future. A less cynical point of view is that by understanding the mistakes of the past, you are likely to know what to avoid. By taking that idea to the next level, if you understand what questions you should be asking yourself, you will probably be better equipped to create, manage, and later modify your portfolio to reduce losses and improve the chances for profit in any market condition.

The five most important questions every investor should ask include the following, which are also summarized in Table 1-2.

QUESTION #1: HOW MUCH RISK, AND WHAT KIND, IS APPROPRIATE FOR ME?

Risk comes in several forms, and in the stock market *awareness* of risk is essential. You cannot simply buy shares of stock because

TABLE 1-2. FIVE QUESTIONS EVERY INVESTOR SHOULD ASK

Question #1: How much risk, and what kind, is appropriate for me?

Question #2: How much do I need to invest today to reach my future goals?

Question #3: What affect will inflation and taxes have on my profits?

Question #4: What strategies are available and which should I use?

Question #5: Should I hire a financial planner or make my own decisions?

someone else does or because you hear a rumor; you need to evaluate market and liquidity risk as well.

Market risk refers to price volatility. The risk that a stock's price will remain flat for a long period of time or worse, decline, is the most obvious and best-known risk for stockholders. It is overcome through diversification and the selection of conservative stocks and by avoiding high-P/E stocks, those higher-risk and more volatile sectors, and unknown, new companies.

Liquidity risk means cash will not be available when you need it or, as an alternative definition, there is no buyer available when you want to sell. In the exchange market, you can always find a buyer for shares, but the price might not be what you want or expect. In some other markets, such as real estate limited partnerships, you do not enjoy a public exchange arena for units you buy, so the only way to sell shares is with a deep discount.

QUESTION #2: HOW MUCH DO I NEED TO INVEST TODAY TO REACH MY FUTURE GOALS?

If you listen to financial advisers, you will hear that you need much more money to retire than you thought, or for college education, paying off your home, or any other future goal. But the estimated future needs analysis often assumes a low return on investments and unrealistically high inflation. Your investment portfolio will not experience the full inflationary rate as long as you don't have to buy a new home and new car every year; a greater inflationary risk is found in the declining value of the dollar, and that is where you need to build your portfolio defensively. But when you consider the dollar amount needed, remember a few points that most financial planners forget to mention: First, you should structure your mortgage so that you own your home free and clear by retirement. This requires careful preplanning and acceleration of payments, as well as the discipline to allow equity to grow and to not refinance.

Second, when you retire you have to consider other sources of income including IRA, company-paid retirement, and social security. In addition, many people retire and reduce their income but continue to work, so don't assume that your income stream will move to zero just because you decide to retire.

And third, any advice you receive from a financial expert has to be taken with one point in mind: The more you invest, the more commission the financial planner receives. (This assumes you work with a commission-based planner, as opposed to one who works for a consulting fee.)

QUESTION #3: WHAT AFFECT WILL INFLATION AND TAXES HAVE ON MY PROFITS?

One invisible factor—overlooked by almost everyone—is the double effect of inflation and taxes. Even though the rate of inflation may be small, the combined impact of these factors is significant on your actual investment return. In other words, it is not enough to break even and it is inadequate to settle for a conservative, safe, but very low return—especially if the after-inflation and after-tax outcome is negative.

To calculate the effect of inflation and taxes, first find the current rate of inflation. You may use the published Consumer Price Index (CPI) reported by the Bureau of Labor Statistics (*www.bls .gov/cpi*, or develop your own personal inflation assumption based on what you believe inflation is going to be for the coming year. The rate you use, expressed as a percentage, is divided by your estimated rate of after-tax income. To find this subtract your *effective tax rate* from 100 percent. This effective rate is the actual percentage you pay in taxes, or your total tax liability divided by your taxable income. Be sure to include both federal and state tax liabilities. The formula:

$$\frac{I}{100-R} = B$$

where I = rate of inflation

R = effective tax rate (federal and state)

B = break-even return

For example, if the current rate of inflation is 3 percent per year and your effective tax rate (federal and state combined) is 34 percent, your break-even return is:

$$\frac{3}{100-34} = 4.5\%$$

This reveals that you need to earn 4.5 percent on your investments just to break even and maintain your purchasing power. If you earn less than 4.5 percent, you are losing money on an after-tax basis. (This calculation is distorted somewhat by tax-free investment income such as qualified dividends and by lower tax rates on capital gains. But the exercise does illustrate the point that a simple rate of return is not always beneficial when taxes and inflation are calculated.) Break-even returns are shown in Table 1-3.

QUESTION #4: WHAT STRATEGIES ARE AVAILABLE AND WHICH SHOULD I USE?

If anything, the modern-day access via the Internet to free advice, strategies, and ideas is an embarrassment of riches.[1] There is so much out there that it is quite difficult to distinguish between the good and the bad. So although there is a lot of free information available today compared to even one decade earlier, you still need to do your homework in order to know how to proceed and which advice to take or reject.

Strategies involve the very beginning decision to employ fundamental or technical analysis, a combination of the two, or to proceed based only on current news and information. Failing to use some type of system and at least a few indicators and trends is a mistake.

TABLE 1-3. BREAK-EVEN RATES

| Effective Tax Rate | I N F L A T I O N   R A T E | | | | | |
	1%	2%	3%	4%	5%	6%
14%	1.2%	2.3%	3.5%	4.7%	5.8%	7.0%
16%	1.2	2.4	3.6	4.8	6.0	7.1
18%	1.2	2.4	3.7	4.9	6.1	7.3
20%	1.3	2.5	3.8	5.0	6.3	7.5
22%	1.3	2.6	3.8	5.1	6.4	7.7
24%	1.3%	2.6%	3.9%	5.3%	6.6%	7.9%
26%	1.4	2.7	4.1	5.4	6.8	8.1
28%	1.4	2.8	4.2	5.6	6.9	8.3
30%	1.4	2.9	4.3	5.7	7.1	8.6
32%	1.5	2.9	4.4	5.9	7.4	8.8
34%	1.5%	3.0%	4.5%	6.1%	7.6%	9.1%
36%	1.6	3.1	4.7	6.3	7.8	9.4
38%	1.6	3.2	4.8	6.5	8.1	9.7
40%	1.7	3.3	5.0	6.7	8.3	10.0
42%	1.7	3.4	5.2	6.9	8.6	10.3

As to how and when you invest, numerous strategies can be used. None ensure profits, but many can add to your self-discipline. For example, you can use dollar cost averaging (also called the constant dollar plan) to place the same amount of money into the market on a periodic basis. Even when share prices rise or fall, dollar cost averaging involves regular investments, often into one stock or mutual fund every week or month.

You can also average up or average down, which may be thought of as the opposite of dollar cost averaging. Under this system, you buy additional shares of stock whenever the share price falls. As a result, your average price is always somewhere between original price and current price. You can also average up, meaning you buy more shares when the share price rises. Under this system, your average price is always higher than the original investment price but lower than current market price. Neither of these systems should be used blindly; you will do better to pick investments based on analysis, and it is always a mistake to blindly put more money into stocks or funds that are not performing well.

Diversification is also a strategy, and it explains why mutual funds are so popular. By definition, a fund holds a diversified portfolio, so you can put very minimal capital amounts into a fund and enjoy broad diversification. However, it is wise to compare costs before picking a fund. A no-load fund has no sales fee, whereas a load fund charges on average 8.5 percent of all money you invest. Other fees may also apply, including an advertising fee (called a 12b.1 fee), back-loads (sales charges taken when you withdraw), and a management fee to compensate the managers who decide what stocks or bonds to buy. An alternative to mutual funds is the exchange-traded fund, or ETF, which needs little or no management. The ETF holds a basket of stocks identified in advance by sector, country, or product and shares can be traded on the open exchange just like stocks, rather than requiring you to buy or sell directly through a fund's management.

You can find out more about mutual funds by going to the industry association Web site, the Investment Company Institute, at *http://www.ici.org.* You can also use a free mutual fund cost calculator to compare one fund to another, available on the SEC Web site, at *http://www.sec.gov/investor/tools/mfcc/mfcc-int.htm.*

QUESTION #5: SHOULD I HIRE A FINANCIAL PLANNER OR MAKE MY OWN DECISIONS?

Most novice investors are timid about the market, and may not be willing to simply jump in without some experience. It seems an obvious choice to hire a financial planner or to work with a brokerage firm offering "full service" in exchange for a high cost to trade. This is ill-advised. The first consideration is that no one will help you to succeed in the market as well as you will help yourself. Financial planners and brokers are commission-compensated salespeople in most instances, so there is an unavoidable conflict of interest. They make money only if you take their advice, and you will discover that this advice usually is to buy products that compensate them. For example, a planner will invariably recommend a load mutual fund, meaning only about $92 out of every $100 you invest goes into the fund; the rest goes for commissions. Another example: A financial planner will rarely, if ever, recommend that you accelerate payments on your mortgage, even though this is sensible for many people. There is no commission paid for giving such advice.

Some financial planners work for a fee. This means you pay by the hour. However, it is possible that the planner *also* gets a commission if you invest in any of the products he or she recommends. While this is double compensation and clearly a conflict, some get around this issue by forming a corporation or separate partnership. So you pay the consultation fee to the planner and the commission goes to the planner's corporation.

Ultimately, you should plan to strike out on your own, make your own decisions, and take complete responsibility for your investment portfolio choices. As a transition between your starting point as a novice and a seasoned investor, you may consider joining an investment club. This is a group of individuals living in the same area who pool their resources and money to pick investments. The history of investment clubs is impressive, and this is a great way to gain real-world experience as an investor. To find out more about forming or joining a local investment club, contact the National Association of Investors Corporation (NAIC) at *http://www.better-investing.org*. You can also find support for your investment program from the American Association of Individual Investors (AAII) at *http://www.aaii.com*.

The overall market can be intimidating at first, but once you step back and look at the big picture, you will begin to see in it a more personalized perspective. Your experience and knowledge grows as you begin to invest, and if you ask the right questions and avoid the pitfalls commonly made, you will be far ahead of the crowd. This process is aided by knowing at least a brief history of the market itself.

A Brief History of the U.S. Stock Market

The "stock market" is not actually a single place, but rather a network of physical and electronic places including buildings, computer centers, and home computers. The origin of the term goes back many hundreds of years when dealers traded shares of stock in person and where the market was, in fact, a physical place.

Many people think of "Wall Street" as the center of the financial universe, and in many respects, that is true. The origin of the name goes back to the early seventeenth century and referred not to a wall, but to a group of people, the Walloons (German-speaking Belgians). New Amsterdam (the original name of New York City) was originally founded by the Walloons; they were instrumental in turning the area into a world port and trade center. The financial center was called "de Waal Straat," or the street where the Walloons conducted business. The settlement was bordered on the north by an actual 12-foot wall, built as a defense against Native Americans, and the British kept the reference to the wall and the street as "Wall Street." Today, the term "Wall Street" refers generally to all business, investment, and commerce and not just to a defensive wall or even simply to the street of the same name.

Two major stock exchanges grew up during the eighteenth century, formalizing trade as volume picked up in the New World. The first and oldest exchange in the United States was the Philadelphia Stock Exchange, founded in 1790. In 1792, a group of merchants in New York organized and formed what later became known as the New York Stock Exchange. Competition between the two exchanges was fierce and the Philadelphia organizers quickly set up a system of telescopes and mirrors by which they could flash signals from New York harbor to Philadelphia in as little as 10 minutes. This amazing system remained in effect until the telegraph was invented in 1846.

The innovation of the communication system is typical of the American Stock Exchange history. The New York, Philadelphia, and American exchanges have always been on the cutting edge of advances, making the most out of the telegraph, ticker, telephone, television, and computer. Each of these technological improvements has created huge leaps in exchange business and in the execution speed of transactions.

It was not always that way. Before the telephone, for example, it was virtually impossible for people to buy and sell shares of stock directly. They had to work through a broker who would go physically to an exchange and transact for them, often for so high a fee that it was not realistic for anyone outside of the brokerage community to try and make money in the stock market.

The history of the stock market is, sadly, a history of greed and of many individuals taking advantage of people and robbing them of their life savings. In addition to the big panics and crashes that have typified the history of the market, a few corrupt individuals also have profited in this environment. Most people today remember Kenneth Lay who, as chief executive officer of Enron, bankrupted the company and its auditor, Arthur Andersen, as a consequence of his creative "incentive pay" and falsified accounting records. That was very recent. But the colorful history of Wall Street has seen many other characters of similar questionable integrity. The well-known market crash of October 1929 led to the formation of the SEC and passage of several important pieces of federal legislation, requiring listed companies to conduct independent audits, meet specific reporting and listing standards, and limiting the kinds of leveraged trading activity that has so often created market crashes in the past. More recently, after the "Enron" period, Congress increased the SEC's enforcement budget and enacted numerous reforms through the Sarbanes–Oxley Act of 2002.

In the past, perhaps the most infamous market con man was Charles Ponzi. The "Ponzi Scheme" is named after him because he operated the sham so effectively. An Italian immigrant who arrived in 1903, Ponzi had a background of minor rackets and schemes meant to take money from people. By 1920, Ponzi had developed the basic idea of his famous scheme: He told would-be investors that if they gave him cash, he guaranteed a 50 percent return in 45 days, 100 percent in 90 days. Few people bothered to ask how he would achieve this because the rate of return was so good, and magic thinking took over from more practical, healthy suspicion. Ponzi ended up with more subscribers and true believers than he could handle. Those who did inquire were told that the idea was based on management of a foreign postal coupon exchange, but few people wanted to ask any in-depth questions, especially because Ponzi's early investors were, indeed, doubling their money every 90 days. Word spread. The scheme was ingenious, simple, and would inevitably fail. As investor numbers increased, Ponzi paid off his initial investors and word continued to spread at an accelerated rate. He finally had to hire agents to handle the volume of people showing up to hand over money. By February 1920, Ponzi was taking in over $5,000 per day. By March, the daily volume had grown to $30,000, and in May it reached $420,000.

So great was the hysteria that people mortgaged their homes and cleaned out their savings to take part in the Ponzi investment. Most did not collect their winnings, but chose to plow their profits back into the plan. Ultimately, the pyramid collapsed because it was built on ever-higher debt. Finally, Ponzi was no longer able to pay off investors and he was sent to prison and then deported to Italy.

The Ponzi scheme demonstrates how many people think. If getting rich sounds too easy, it is probably some kind of a scheme, but people want to believe. They allow their own greed to overrule their judgment, and like the Ponzi investors they end up losing thousands, perhaps millions.

On a larger scale, markets have risen and fallen over time, and landmark dates in market history are often the big crashes. Today, the Internet has made the stock market more efficient than ever and has also made stockbrokers virtually obsolete. Traders do not need to telephone a broker and pay exorbitant fees to execute trades; they can do it themselves from their own home or office computer. Unfortunately, this low-cost convenience also has made it easier for con artists to find their victims, and has made market crashes faster and more devastating than ever. With over 26 million computers in use around the world, the stock market today does not exist only in a physical sense in lower Manhattan; it is truly a worldwide market. The New York Stock Exchange (NYSE), only one of many exchanges around the world, transactions more than $2 trillion every trading day.

The big market crashes in U.S. history are worth summarizing, as these define the history of the stock market, often resulting from economic recessions or from the abuses of individuals. The nine worst, based on declines in the Dow Jones Industrial Average (DJIA), were:

1. April 17, 1930 to July 8, 1932 (loss: 86%)
2. March 10, 1939 to March 31, 1908 (loss: 49%)
3. January 1, 1906 to November 15, 1907 (loss: 49%)
4. September 3, 1929 to November 13, 1929 (loss: 48%)
5. November 3, 1919 to August 24, 1921 (loss: 47%)
6. June 17, 1901 to November 9, 1903 (loss: 46%)
7. September 12, 1939 to April 4, 1942 (loss: 40%)
8. November 21, 1916 to December 19, 1917 (loss: 40%)
9. January 15, 2002 to October 9, 2002 (the DJIA lost 38% of its value)

This list provides perspective to the modern versions of stock market crashes. Note that the 1987 crash of over 500 points did not even make the list, and the very brief decline in value following 9/11 was so minor it was not even considered a crash.

This all raises an important question: Why do crashes and panics happen? Some important things to remember about the market:

1. *Price levels always come back from declines, although it often takes time.* This works in both directions, as history reveals. No price trends move in one direction forever. However, over time, values of listed companies, overall, have increased. Capital is not finite, and capitalism creates wealth. The stock market is an extraordinary form of freedom, where you can place capital at risk and watch it appreciate over time. The occasional price plunges invariably return to previous levels. The key is that if you pick stocks intelligently, a market-wide price decline does not permanently affect the value of your investment. Even when prices fall, they will rise again.

2. *The market overreacts to everything.* In fact, crashes themselves are forms of severe overreaction. In a sensible, logical, and stable world prices would simply rise gradually over time. For example, look at the real estate market. In spite of the price and credit bubble of recent years, the history of real estate shows that in most regions, prices steadily increase over time. Even during the bubble, the problems were isolated to a few states where past abuses were

most severe and where prices had run up beyond reason. So if you exclude California, Arizona, and Florida from the national averages, even during the 2004–2007 bubble years, the overall price of real estate in the United States remained very steady with prices trending up and down within normal cycles.

The stock market is an exciting, high-risk market. You can double your money in a matter of hours or weeks, but you can also lose half of it in the same time if you take too high a risk. That would be unlikely in the real estate market. The stock market tends to rise and fall in extreme degrees because of its liquidity and ease of trading, and because of the tendency for individuals, analysts, and institutional investors to take all news and exaggerate it, both positively and negatively.

3. *No matter how much analysis you perform, the market contains many unknown factors and is impossible to anticipate.* This is the simple reality. Even so, many "systems" can be found to beat the market. None of them work consistently, but you can vastly improve your odds by performing your own analysis and making smart choices. It is the unknown factor that adds so much value to stocks. Much of today's price and price movement occurs in anticipation of things that have not yet occurred, such as future earnings, possible mergers and acquisitions, labor strikes, development of new products and new markets, and changes in the competition. No one can anticipate what is going to happen next year or even next week and this uncertainty adds to both risk and to potential reward in the market.

History demonstrates extreme price swings in the market. Following some price crashes, it has taken many years for the market value to return to previous levels. But for the most part, the market tends to recover quickly, especially in stocks whose fundamental value is strong and does not change. Such a company may see its stock price plummet with the rest of the market. But the stronger the company, the faster its price will rebound after a crash.

You can also learn a lot from history about the difficulty of finding easy money. The long history of con games and swindles, both by individuals and insiders, serves as an important lesson. There is

no easy money! Many people will appeal to greed and rob unsus-
pecting investors of their life savings, but everyone should know
better. If there were easy paths to riches, strangers would not be so
willing to share their secrets with you. So any time someone offers
to help you double your money, keep one hand on your wallet and
never give out information. One thing that is sure in the market:
Giving money to anyone making such promises is a sure thing, on
the losing side.

Note

1   From the French, *L'Embarras des richesses* 1726 play tr. by John Ozell in 1738,
    meaning an abundance of something beyond what is needed.

THE BOTTOM LINE

M ost experts agree that corporate earnings (expressed as earnings per share, or EPS) are one of the key factors in studying stocks. This is especially true when tracked over time, as part of a growing and emerging trend. Looking at EPS by itself reveals nothing, because earnings vary based on the number of shares outstanding.

This chapter explains EPS and market price in the context of how you can use the information to study a company's performance. This requires developing historical trends as well as projections of the future. EPS should be studied for each company in this manner, and the growth curve should be studied and compared to other stocks in the same industry or sector.

Price is a separate but equally important factor, although it has nothing directly to do with the fundamentals. The price per share of stock reflects the current perception of value, which factors in expectations about future growth. It is a common mistake to view market price as being associated with financial information but, in fact, price *is* perception.

One of the more popular market measurements is the price-to-earnings (P/E) ratio. Although higher P/E most often is seen as reflecting higher market popularity, long-term studies reveal that lower-P/E stocks outperform market averages. Many investors need to reexamine their opinion of P/E. This chapter also warns that the older the earnings information, the less reliable the P/E because outdated earnings per share are being compared to current market prices.

The Corporate Income Statement

What exactly does it mean when a company reports its *earnings*? If you ask this question of others, you soon discover that people have vastly different perceptions about what earnings represent. Some believe earnings are the same as revenue or that earnings and profits are always the same number. In fact, the definition of earnings is more complex than this.

The way that companies report profit and loss makes earnings somewhat more elusive than most people would like. Figure 2-1 summarizes and defines the various segments of the income statement, ending with net earnings.

A few important points to make about reading financial statements:

1. Dollar amounts are usually reported in millions of dollars, unless otherwise qualified. For example, $1,000 would actually represent $1 million or $1 billion. This is commonly used shorthand for the purpose of reporting to stockholders.

2. While the format of the income statement follows a general consistency, the terminology is not always identical. It varies by industry and by type of activity. For example, many companies divide general expenses into two groups: general and administrative (G&A) and selling expenses. The top line, revenues, may be given a different name or defined by type. For example, a company making a lot of revenue from interest income may break out a separate line to distinguish interest from other revenues.

3. The reporting method for companies is at times not as detailed as you might expect. Even in the annual report, where a lot of detail is desirable, some companies provide only a highly summa-

FIGURE 2.1. THE INCOME STATEMENT

Gross revenue		xxx,xxx,xxx
Less: returns and allowances		x,xxx
Net revenue		xxx,xxx,xxx
Cost of goods sold:		
Beginning inventory	xx,xxx,xxx	
Materials purchased	xxx,xxx,xxx	
Direct labor	xx,xxx,xxx	
Other direct costs	x,xxx,xxx	
Subtotal	xxx,xxx,xxx	
Less: ending inventory	xx,xxx,xxx	
Cost of goods sold		xxx,xxx,xxx
Gross profit		xx,xxx,xxx
General expenses		xx,xxx,xxx
Operating profit		xx,xxx,xxx
Plus: other income		x,xxx,xxx
Less: other expenses		(x,xxx,xxx)
Pre-tax profit		xx,xxx,xxx
Federal income taxes		x,xxx,xxx
After-tax net profit		xx,xxx,xxx

rized financial report. So even with the uniformity of reporting under accounting standards, it is not always easy to make company-to-company comparisons.

4. Companies sometimes have to "restate" past reports. This occurs when mistakes were made and later have to be fixed, or when an operating unit is sold. In the interest of consistency and accu-

racy, past reports are changed to reflect current reports. For example, if a company has been overstating net profits and the latest year's audits reflect that, previous net profit reports will be altered. And if a company sells one of its major operating units, previous reports are restated to show profits without that unit. In this way, you can look at all lines of the income statement for many years and get an accurate picture of how trends have moved over time.

5. Income statements are summaries of activity for a very specific period of time, usually the latest fiscal quarter or fiscal year. "Fiscal" simply means the reporting period chosen by the company. While most individuals use the calendar year for reporting and paying taxes, corporations can elect to have their fiscal year end on any month. Based on the industry, there are strategic reasons for picking one fiscal year over another. When a report is provided for the latest quarter, it is compared to the same quarter in the previous fiscal year, so that the comparison is meaningful. A full year's report is usually shown in two columns: the current year and the previous year.

In Figure 2-1, the specific lines and their meanings are:

Gross revenue is the dollar value of sales, unadjusted, made during a specific period, usually a full fiscal year or the latest quarter.

Returns and allowances are adjustments to revenue for discounts, merchandise returns, rebates, and refunds.

Net revenue is the net of gross revenue, minus returns and allowances.

Cost of goods sold is broadly defined as costs directly associated with the generation of revenue. For example, when a company buys merchandise it is bought at wholesale and sold at marked-up value or retail. Merchandise is a direct cost, because the amount of revenue and the cost of merchandise are related. In comparison, expenses like rent, telephone, or clerical salaries will remain at the same level whether revenue rises or falls.

With the cost of goods sold, several line items occur. The inventory, or goods kept on hand in warehouses or stores, or in plants where manufacturing and assembly take place, is adjusted within cost of goods sold. The net change between beginning inventory (cost value at the beginning of the period) and ending inventory (cost value at the end of the period) is one form of adjustment. The direct cost is increased by materials purchased during the year, direct labor (the cost of manufacture and assembly, for example), and other line items like freight and other costs needed to get merchandise sold.

The total of all direct costs, including increase or decrease in inventory levels, is the cost of goods sold. This is deducted from net revenue.

Gross profit is the remaining value of net revenues minus the cost of goods sold.

General expenses includes all overhead and other expenses the company pays each year. This includes nondirect salaries and wages, payroll taxes, retirement benefits, insurance, rent, telephone, office supplies, advertising, and dozens of other categories. The main distinction between costs and expenses is whether it is related to production of revenue. Payment of rent is required whether revenue rises or falls, so it is an expense. Purchases of merchandise for resale is clearly a direct cost; it rises as the volume of sales grows, and falls if and when sales decline.

Operating profit is the net of earnings (profit) strictly from operating the company. In other words, if the company did not need to spend money on nonoperating expenses or pay taxes, this would be the "bottom line." But there are more adjustments.

Other income is a nonoperating item. It includes gains from selling capital assets or operating units, foreign exchange gains, winnings from lawsuits, and interest.

Other expenses include nonoperating losses, such as losses on the sale of capital assets, legal judgments paid, foreign exchange losses, and interest expenses.

Pre-tax profit represents earnings from both operating and nonoperating activities before adjusting for tax liabilities.

Federal income taxes includes the allowance added for the current year's tax liability based on taxable corporate income.

After-tax net profit is the bottom line; the net earnings of the company after all sources of income, costs, and expenses are taken into account.

The Attributes of Earnings

Knowing the general definitions used on the income statement is a wise starting point. If you are not sure what "earnings" really means, it is impossible to make valid comparisons between companies or between quarters or years. Definition is the starting point in knowing how to evaluate a company *before* buying stock.

Earnings contain specific attributes based on the industry and the company. It is unrealistic to expect any company's *net return* to rise every year and indefinitely into the future. The dollar value should rise as sales rise, but the net return—the percentage of net earnings divided by revenue—should remain consistent.

The formula for net return is summarized in Figure 2-2.

For example, three listed corporations report vastly different net returns over five years. Table 2-1 shows these results.

It is always interesting to compare net return on two different levels: first, the trend within the company, and second, outcomes between companies. These three corporations are in completely different industries, so a standard for net return cannot be applied equally to each. Rather, outcomes should be compared between a company and its direct competitors, those corporations operating in the same business.

This comparison is interesting, however, because as a prelimi-

FIGURE 2.2. NET RETURN

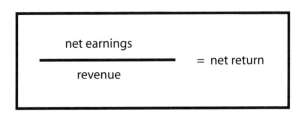

$$\frac{\text{net earnings}}{\text{revenue}} = \text{net return}$$

TABLE 2-1. NET RETURN COMPARISONS

Company	Year	In Millions of Dollars		Net Return
		Revenue	Net Profit	
AT&T	2006	$ 63,055	$ 7,356	11.7%
	2005	43,862	4,786	10.9
	2004	40,787	4,979	12.2
	2003	40,843	5,971	14.6
	2002	43,138	7,473	17.3
Citigroup	2006	$146,558	$21,249	14.5%
	2005	120,318	19,806	16.5
	2004	108,276	17,046	15.7
	2003	94,713	17,853	18.8
	2002	92,556	13,448	14.5
IBM	2006	$ 91,424	$ 9,416	10.3%
	2005	91,134	7,994	8.8
	2004	96,293	8,448	8.8
	2003	89,131	7,613	8.5
	2002	81,186	5,334	6.6

Source: Standard & Poor's Stock Reports

nary method for picking companies as investments, it demonstrates several basic but important positive points, including:

1. The companies were profitable each year in the analysis.
2. Changes from year to year are not highly volatile, meaning that year-to-year revenue, net income, and net return are somewhat predictable.
3. Revenue is shown for each of the companies during the five years.

A more specific analysis shows that results are actually mixed, even though revenue rose in each case. AT&T (T) experienced significant increases in revenue, although its net income declined for the first four of the five years. This is further reflected in net return, which also declined throughout the period. This does not mean the company is heading into bankruptcy, but it does raise questions. Why is net return declining in a period when revenue rose? It usually means that expenses are rising or that, due to competition, costs (and thus, profit margin) are squeezed. In either case, the trend is worth further study.

Citigroup (C) experienced substantial rise in both revenue and net income. Its net return began and ended the period at 14.5 percent, with higher net return in between. This probably reflects the changing financial markets in 2003 through 2005, more than any management issues or competitive changes within the company. In 2007, Citigroup's fortunes were more dismal.

IBM (IBM) also experienced strong growth both in revenue and net income. Its net return rose strongly through the five years, indicating improving margins as well as continued controls over expense levels. Although IBM's net return is lower than the two other companies in this study, it does not reflect a negative. Every industry is different, and this simply indicates that the gross margins for IBM are different than for AT&T and Citigroup. For example, IBM manufactures and sells hardware so it has inventory costs as well as direct labor. In comparison, both AT&T and Citigroup focus more on services and, in the case of Citigroup, interest income. The margin from this kind of activity is invariably higher than for corporations selling products. This makes the point that comparisons between industries are not valid. A valid comparison would be to contrast IBM to other information technology (IT) hardware manufacturers and Citigroup to other financial institutions.

Tracking Earnings Per Share Over Time

The net income reported by a company is a dollar value but analysis often takes place in shorthand. Even the dollar values leave off six zeroes by reporting in millions of dollars. Earnings (net income) are commonly reported not by dollar value but by earnings per share (EPS).

There is a good reason for this. If one company has 10 million shares outstanding and another has 20 million, an identical dollar value of net income has vastly different significance on a per-share basis—regardless of the percentage of net return. EPS is also significant because corporate shares outstanding may change over time. In an ideal situation, issuing more shares translates to higher EPS because the infusion of new capital enables the company to grow over time.

It is also important to recognize a trend among large listed companies to buy and retire its own shares on the market, and the effect this has on EPS. When a company buys its own shares it is a positive sign that management believes the stock is a bargain at its current price. When it buys those shares, the company retires them permanently. So if earnings are exactly the same from one year to the next, but the company buys a large portion of its outstanding shares and retires them, this will *increase* EPS.

The calculation of EPS involves dividing earnings by the number of outstanding shares. Earnings cover one full year, so the calculation needs to be adjusted if and when the number of shares changes. For example, if the company bought (and retired) shares during the year, the number of average shares outstanding has to be adjusted to make the calculation accurate. And if the company issued new shares during the year, that also has to be taken into account in calculating EPS.

A word on modifying the outstanding shares: The calculation has to include a weighting for the months specific numbers of shares were outstanding. For example, if a company started the year with 9 million shares and bought and retired 150,000 shares at the beginning of the third month of its fiscal year, it would have to calculate the average shares as follows:

2 months, 9 million shares outstanding

10 months, 8.85 million shares outstanding

average shares outstanding:

$$2/12 \times 9.00 \text{ million} = 1.50$$
$$10/12 \times 8.85 \text{ million} = 7.37$$
$$\text{total} = 8.87 \text{ million shares}$$

This is the number of shares outstanding to be used in calculating EPS. The calculation involves dividing earnings by the number of shares outstanding. This formula is summarized in Figure 2-3.

For example, returning to the previous example of AT&T, Citigroup, and IBM, earnings per share is a revealing analytical tool. The real meaning of earnings is more significant when analyzed on a per-share basis than on the dollar value of net return, as shown in Table 2-2.

The EPS for AT&T has declined over the five years in question, so on this basis performance has been disappointing. Citigroup, in comparison, experienced a steady rise in EPS, and IBM's performance was even stronger. From an investor's point of view, which attempts to place value on the revenue and earnings trend, an EPS analysis over at least five years is the best procedure to follow.

You might expect price performance to track EPS, or in other words, as EPS improves, the stock's price range should climb as well. This is a reasonable assumption, although outside conditions affect price range as well. The general condition of the market for a particular industry will keep prices down even as EPS rises, or vice versa. However, it is interesting to study the price ranges for a period of time compared to EPS. A summary is shown in Table 2-3.

The comparison reveals that you cannot rely solely on EPS to predict market share. Over a long period of time, prices will rise for corporations whose earnings and EPS rise, but in the short term it is more elusive. In the case of AT&T, the low price rose during the five years while the high price in the range fell. This makes sense when you also observe the decline in EPS over the same period. The

FIGURE 2.3. EARNINGS PER SHARE (EPS)

$$\frac{\text{net earnings}}{\text{shares outstanding}} = \text{EPS}$$

TABLE 2-2. EARNINGS PER SHARE (EPS)

Company	Year	In Millions Net Profit	In Millions Shares Outstanding	EPS
AT&T	2006	$ 7,356	3,902	$1.89
	2005	4,786	3,379	1.42
	2004	4,979	3,322	1.50
	2003	5,971	3,329	1.80
	2002	7,473	3,351	2.23
Citigroup	2006	$21,249	5,000	$4.25
	2005	19,806	5,185	3.82
	2004	17,046	5,229	3.26
	2003	17,853	5,220	3.42
	2002	13,448	5,200	2.59
IBM	2006	$ 9,416	1,554	$6.06
	2005	7,994	1,628	4.91
	2004	8,448	1,710	4.94
	2003	7,613	1,754	4.34
	2002	5,334	1,737	3.07

Source: Standard & Poor's Stock Reports

Citigroup history makes sense. The low price levels nearly doubled, even though the high price range showed less growth. The case of IBM is more puzzling: While the low price range went up substantially, the high price actually fell (even though EPS doubled during the period). This could indicate that the stock was undervalued at the end of fiscal 2006, with a high price of only $98. In fact, 10 months into 2007, IBM stock was selling above $115 per share. This level of growth makes more sense given the change in revenue, earnings, and EPS over the previous five years.

The lesson from this analysis is clear: You can use net return and EPS to pick stocks. The recent history may confirm what you see in price trends, or price trends may be lagging behind, pointing to possible bargains in the market. The case of IBM is a good example of this, with a falling high price trend over five years through

TABLE 2-3. EPS AND SHARE PRICE RANGE

| | | | Share Price Range | |
Company	Year	EPS	Low	High
AT&T	2006	$1.89	$24	$36
	2005	1.42	22	26
	2004	1.50	23	28
	2003	1.80	19	32
	2002	2.23	20	41
Citigroup	2006	$4.25	$ 45	$57
	2005	3.82	43	50
	2004	3.26	42	53
	2003	3.42	30	49
	2002	2.59	24	52
IBM	2006	$6.06	$ 73	$ 98
	2005	4.91	72	99
	2004	4.94	91	100
	2003	4.34	73	95
	2002	3.07	54	126

Source: Standard & Poor's Stock Reports

2006, which improved into 2007. However, conditions in market-wide trends also affect these stock price ranges, so that is only one piece of the puzzle.

Core Earnings

Net income is supposed to accurately reflect the operational outcome for a company. Unfortunately, accounting rules are very liberal, and corporations often include in "net income" some forms of income that are not recurring and not even related directly to their primary business.

Standard & Poor's (S&P), which rates corporate creditworthiness, devised a system for adjusting net income to fix this problem. The corporate *core earnings* is an adjusted version of net income that removes noncore income. It also puts expenses into the picture that may have been excluded from the conventional accounting reports.

Core earnings should track reported net income fairly closely and, in fact, in well-managed companies core earnings are very close to "net income." But in some other companies, a lot of variation is found between net income and core earnings. It often is accompanied with a lot of volatility in the numbers, with revenue and net income changing from one year to the next. Volatility in the financial statements makes it very difficult to predict future growth levels, so that alone is a troubling sign. When you also see chronic large adjustments between reporting earnings and core earnings, it is even worse. A one-time adjustment can be expected if an unusual occurrence is in play, such as the sale of a large operating unit or an accounting restatement. But when core earnings adjustments are substantial every year, it indicates that there is a larger problem in the way the company is reporting its profits and losses.

You will discover a correlation between core earnings adjustments and the stock price over a period of time. The more volatile the year-to-year financial reports and core earnings adjustments, the more volatile the stock price will be. Those companies reporting very little in the way of core earnings adjustments will also tend to reflect long-term price appreciation and low volatility on the technical side (price movement)—not always, but often.

A comparison of three corporations' net income and core earnings demonstrates not only the variety of outcomes, but the significance that these adjustments can and do make. Table 2-4 shows these results for a five-year period.

These results summarize a range of possible core earnings adjustments. McDonald's (MCD) reported relatively minor adjustments each year, reducing net income from a high of $325 million in the earliest year to only $25 million in the latest. Because core earnings track net income fairly closely and the trend is in the same direction for both, these adjustments are not troubling.

In comparison, Du Pont de Nemours (DD) also reported rising net profits and core earnings but the level of annual adjustments is far higher, and two of the five years showed core earnings higher

TABLE 2-4. NET INCOME AND CORE EARNINGS

| Company | Year | In Millions of Dollars | | |
		Net Profit	Core Earnings	Adjustment
McDonald's	2006	$ 2,873	$ 2,848	$ – 25
	2005	2,602	2,540	– 64
	2004	2 279	2,100	– 179
	2003	1,508	1,226	– 282
	2002	992	667	– 325
Du Pont de Nemours	2006	$ 3,148	$ 2,768	$ – 380
	2005	2,053	1,965	– 88
	2004	1,780	2,008	228
	2003	1,002	1,132	130
	2002	1,841	398	– 1,443
General Motors	2006	$ – 1,978	$ 1,972$	3,950
	2005	– 10,458	– 6,741	3,717
	2004	2,805	4,040	1,235
	2003	2,862	4,510	1,648
	2002	1,736	– 838	– 2,574

Source: Standard & Poor's Stock Reports

than net income. The earliest year had a negative adjustment of $1.443 *billion*. This level of adjustment is very troubling. Net income was reported at $1.841 billion, but core earnings were only $398 million. Even the latest reported year, with a downward adjustment of $380 million, represented 12 percent of total net income.

General Motors (GM) was the most troubling of the three. Every year showed adjustments between net income and core earnings of more than $1 billion. The two latest years approached $4 billion, which is massive. Even though four of the five years showed an increase between net and core, this level of adjustment is disturbing. It points out the flaws of the accounting rules, which allow companies to report so inaccurately that this level of adjustment between net income and core earnings is needed. The fact that the problem is chronic in the case of GM raises another question: Why does the company continue to report net income in the manner it does, and why are so many adjustments required?

Each case should be investigated to determine the reasons for core earnings adjustments, especially when they are so large. In GM's case, these adjustments were the result of what the company called "special attribution" and "restructuring and impairment charges." These references involve accounting decisions due to losses in primary manufacturing as well as the parts business, and obvious disagreement between GM's auditors and S&P's (the company that defines and calculates core earnings). The fact that these differences have not been resolved indicates that similar very large adjustments are also likely to recur in the future. From the point of view of the investor or analyst considering whether to buy a company's stock, this level of uncertainty is very troubling. The problems GM faces are severe and more will be explained in a later chapter. The point to remember here is that the huge adjustments to arrive at core earnings serve as a warning that more is wrong in the financial results.[1]

Core Earnings Basics

The concept of core earnings has only been around since 2002, so long-term comparisons between reports and core earnings are limited. However, the comparison for the years the data have been published can be very valuable.

The primary core earnings adjustments include two broad categories: first are items to be included in earnings that are often left out, and second are items to be excluded that companies often leave in.

ITEMS INCLUDED IN CORE EARNINGS

Employee stock option grants are benefits given to top executives and other employees. The options allow the employee to buy shares of the company's stock at a fixed price as long as those options are exercised by a specified date in the future. The problem with this benefit is that in the past, options were given out but never placed anywhere on the books as expenses. They were explained in footnotes only. So when an executive exercised the options, the effect was to dilute the value of all other shares, but without ever recording the expenses. Standard & Poor's correctly pegged stock options as a current-year expense, one that artificially bolstered reported profits. As a form of compensation, these options are properly reported as expenses in the year they are granted, even if they are not exercised until many years in the future.

Restructuring charges is a fancy way of describing "cutting back" on expenses, usually involving closing down plants and laying off employees. It sounds more esoteric, but it simply is an admission that the company is too big or unable to compete on the scale of its previous size. Companies have expenses associated with this "restructuring," such as severance pay to laid-off employees. S&P has identified these as current-year expenses. Companies have preferred to capitalize these expenses and amortize them over a number of years, but that is inaccurate.

Write-down of assets are reductions in value. This is accomplished normally by way of depreciation and amortization, but some assets simply lose value above and beyond those periodic charges. Companies often capitalized these reduced values as a form of additional amortization, but under the core earnings interpretation, they should be included in current-year expenses.

Pension costs are among the largest expenditures some companies have each year. Under an oddity of accounting, these costs were simply excluded from the operating reports, as though providing pension benefits did not relate to current year activity. Core earnings adjusts the profit and loss in those instances to reduce profits by the amount of pension costs. This is especially appropriate because many companies prefer to exclude costs while improperly including estimated pension profits (see items excluded below).

Research and development (R&D) bought by the company are also included as current-year expenses and not amortized over many years. It is a favorite trick under the accounting rules to spread expenses out over several years to keep profits high, but when a company buys R&D, core earnings rules state that those expenses are to be included in the year the expenses are incurred.

ITEMS EXCLUDED FROM CORE EARNINGS

Goodwill impairment is somewhat technical, but it is worth a brief explanation. "Goodwill" is an intangible asset, an estimate of a company's value above and beyond its buildings, equipment, and other physical assets. When a company buys a competitor, for example, it may overpay to close the deal. The definition of goodwill is the net difference between the price the acquiring company paid and the tangible value of assets. "Impairment" is an expense by which companies reduce the goodwill asset to reflect diminished value. Under the core earnings rules, impairment cannot be counted as a current-year expense. The rule is fair: An intangible asset is booked with no tangible asset to back it up, so reducing its value to create a current-year expense is not allowed. (Remember, however, that core earnings are simply an estimate restatement of income and expenses, and not a *change* in the tax-based report issued by the company. Core earnings simply is an attempt to adjust profit and loss to reflect outcome for the primary business of the company.)

Gains or losses from the sale of capital assets are forms of income not related to the primary business. Capital assets—buildings, trucks and autos, office and manufacturing equipment, and so on—are normally capitalized or set up as assets and depreciated over several years. At the point these assets are sold, the difference between sale price and book value (price less depreciation) is a net profit or loss. However, these gains and losses are not part of core earnings. The same rule applies when companies sell operating units, which may change net profit by billions of dollars. It is nonrecurring, however, and cannot be called a part of current-year profits.

Pension gains are an oddity in accounting. A *pro forma* number is created to estimate gains based on investment activity, and these gains are often far from accurate or are difficult to pin down. Because the gains are unrealized and based on estimates, they are excluded. Even realized pension gains are not part of the current-year income of the company.

Gains and losses from hedging activities that have not been realized are also excluded. An unrealized gain or loss is one existing on paper, just as ownership of stock with value higher or lower than original cost is not counted until sold. Companies use available cash to invest in the market through hedging, but any unsold asset gains or losses cannot be counted under core earnings rules.

Merger and acquisition (M&A) expenses are often the subject of accounting manipulation. Depending on the timing of when these expenses are booked or how the deal is put together, M&A expenses have been used in the past to artificially inflate net profits or defer tax liabilities. Under the core earnings rules, expenses of acquiring other companies are left off of the profit and loss summary.

Litigation or insurance settlements or proceeds can be substantial, either as forms of income or as expenses. In either case, they are nonrecurring and are not part of the current-year primary (core) earnings. When companies include these in the income statement, they are removed to arrive at core earnings.

The Price-Earnings Ratio

The fact that core earnings adjustments have often been substantial is troubling to anyone depending on fundamental analysis to pick stocks. If, in fact, core earnings adjustments are large (either upward or downward) then all profit-based ratios will be distorted. While company-to-company comparisons are valuable, they become questionable when the core earnings are not similar. For example, if one company has little or no adjustments and another has very large adjustments, they cannot be compared accurately.

There is self-deception involved in using traditional but inflexible models for stocks. Favorite ratios like the price-earnings (P/E) ratio are obviously going to be distorted whenever net profits are adjusted, at times in the billions of dollars. So a P/E ratio has to be valued with potential core earnings in mind; when core earnings adjustments are significant, the P/E should be viewed with that qualification. However, because P/E is so widely used and invariably based on net income (and not on core earnings), it is difficult to apply a revised standard universally. It is prudent, however, to be aware of the level of core earnings adjustments and to analyze P/E on an adjusted basis—core P/E—whenever adjustments are substantial.

The P/E is easy to calculate. Price per share is divided by earnings per share (EPS); the formula is summarized in Figure 2-4.

For example, a stock sells today at $55.00 per share, and latest reported EPS was $4.55. So P/E is:

$$\frac{\$55.00}{\$4.55} = 12$$

The P/E is always expressed as a single numerical value called the *multiple*. It is commonly rounded to the closest whole number. So in this example, the multiple is 12, meaning the stock is selling at 12 times earnings.

In studying P/E, it is reliable to study the P/E range over a period of years and to also review year-end price and earnings. Otherwise, the ratio is distorted. For example, if you look at today's price and compare it to the latest-known EPS, you could be distorting the ratio. If EPS is two months old and the price has changed considerably since that latest quarterly report, P/E in its current form is not a reliable indicator.

Table 2-5 shows the five-year range of P/E for three companies. It is valuable to compare these and interpret what the P/E reveals.

FIGURE 2.4. PRICE/EARNINGS RATIO (P/E)

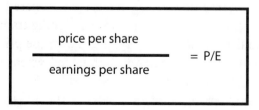

TABLE 2-5. PRICE-EARNINGS RATIOS

Company	Year	High P/E	Low P/E
Merck (MRK)	2006	23	16
	2005	17	12
	2004	19	10
	2003	22	14
	2002	21	12
JPMorgan Chase (JPM)	2006	12	9
	2005	17	14
	2004	28	22
	2003	12	6
	2002	50	19
Starbucks (SBUX)	2006	55	39
	2005	53	37
	2004	68	35
	2003	50	29
	2002	48	34

Source: Standard & Poor's Stock Reports

These historical P/E levels and trends are quite different from one another, and they are also very revealing. In picking stocks to buy or determining whether to hold or sell, it is useful to employ several ratios; however, just by looking at the P/E you can conclude a lot about each of these companies.

Merck reported a historically low P/E range as well as consistency. This is desirable because it implies not only low volatility, but very steady growth in earnings and in price. In comparison, JPMorgan Chase (JPM) has been quite volatile, although its P/E range has come down over five years, which is positive. The large changes in the first three years were significant, but since then the range and level have both calmed down. Starbucks has reported consistently high P/E; even its annual low P/E range has been high at over 21 in February 2008 (see table). For anyone looking for stocks with bargain-level multiples, Starbucks is too expensive. One of two things would need to occur: Earnings would have to grow considerably without a corresponding change in price range, or the price would have to fall.

| | Starbucks P/E Ranges | |
Year	Low	High
2007	23	42
2006	39	55
2005	37	53
2004	35	68
2003	29	50

Source: Standard & Poor's Stock Reports.

P/E is, and should be, a favorite ratio for valuing stocks, and it is simple to comprehend. In determining whether a stock is relatively cheap, the P/E is the most reliable tool. P/E is an important test of value, and the following points should be remembered:

1. *P/E is a reliable value test.* In identifying bargains, P/E helps as a comparative test. The higher the P/E, the greater the likelihood that the stock is too expensive. A very high P/E translates to higher than average risk. A "typical" P/E is a matter of opinion, but most well-priced stocks offer P/E between 10 and 25. So for many investors, comparative P/E analysis is one method for narrowing down a list of potential investments.

2. *P/E is easy to understand and compare.* Unlike some rather esoteric ratios, P/E is simple. It is useful for tracking one company's stock over time as well as for making comparisons between different stocks.

3. *Your decisions are made easier using P/E.* Investors struggle with the question of when (and if) to buy, as well as whether to hold or sell stocks. A basis has to be used for making decisions to cut losses or to take profits, or even to continue holding a stock. The P/E can be used to set a standard. For example, if P/E rises, it indicates that the stock is overpriced compared to its previous price

levels. This does *not* necessarily mean that the stock's market price has risen; it could mean that the earnings have declined. Even when price remains at the same level, if earnings per share decline, then P/E will rise.

The problem of core earnings remains. If the difference between reported net profit and adjusted core earnings is large, then P/E will be distorted. This is especially true in those cases where core earnings adjustments are erratic. When adjustments occur in the billions of dollars, often replacing reported profits with core net losses, the P/E as reported clearly cannot be depended upon for year-to-year or company-to-company analysis.

Adjustments between reported net income and core earnings not only affect investor decisions concerning portfolio holdings, they also affect market perceptions of a stock's value as an investment. At the same time, the items adjusted to reflect only core earnings remain valid adjustments for companies; they are just not part of the core earnings, meaning they cannot be expected to recur.

Ultimately, the real "value" of a company is what it would be worth if it were liquidated today. This *enterprise value* consists of the net value of the company if it were to be liquidated entirely. This excludes intangible assets and recognizes the claims of both equity investors (stockholders) and debt investors (bondholders and other lenders).

The valuation of a company is a difficult and elusive matter. Accounting rules are complex enough so that no one has an easy task trying to compare one organization to another, or even to get a reliable picture of what happens in one company from year to year. Because fundamental transactions and reports affect the stock price, it is far too difficult for anyone to simply determine whether a company's current price is a good bargain. This is why the basic P/E continues to serve as a reliable and worthwhile indicator. Core earnings in many cases make only an insignificant difference in P/E, so perhaps the smartest way to evaluate stocks is to first eliminate those companies with excessively large core earnings adjustments, and then make P/E comparisons over several years and among several companies.

The next chapter takes this discussion to another level, the current yield. This comes from dividends the company declares and pays. For many investors, dividend income is going to act as a significant portion of total income, but this aspect of total return is often overlooked or discounted by investors more intrigued by day-to-day market price action.

Note

1   As of the end of 2006, General Motors reported *negative* net worth of $5.441 billion, and total long-term debt at 115% of total capitalization. Source: GM annual statement, at *www.gm.com*.

YIELD AND
YIELD HISTORY

W hat is dividend yield and how can it be used to judge and compare stocks? This chapter explains dividends and historical yield as a means for judging stability and fundamental strength. It also explains why yield as reported in the financial press is deceptive. The press reports yield as a percentage of the stock's current price; investors should track yield based on their purchase price only, because market price is changing constantly.

Misconceptions about yield abound. The investor has to remember that rate of return varies depending upon how many months or years an investment is owned. This chapter explains how yield and return work and how yield differs from earnings—in other words, how net earnings as a percentage of sales is vastly different than the combination of dividend yield on invested capital plus capital gains. Because investors tend to obscure the difference, it is necessary to mark the distinction in order to clarify all comparisons.

Dividends as a Form of Income

It is easy to overlook, or even ignore, dividends when picking and comparing stocks. The yield is quite small in terms of percentages and dollar value, so does the dividend really mean much at all? Dividend yield is one of the more important criteria for choosing companies as investments for several reasons:

1. *Dividends are a form of income.* Over many years, a persistent stream of current income adds up. As a segment of retirement income, dividends can play a major role, so having a portfolio of safe, high-yielding stocks is a smart long-term plan.

2. *Reinvested dividends provide compound rates of return.* Taking dividends in cash makes no sense until you plan to actually use the dividend income for monthly expenses. While building wealth over many years, reinvested dividends create a powerful form of compound returns. Not only do you earn "dividends on dividends" from buying partial shares every quarter, those increased holdings also offer the potential for capital gains in the future. The more dividends reinvested, the more you earn and the more additional shares you receive.

3. *A company's ability to pay and increase dividends is a critical test of sound management.* As one important test of a company's ability to manage its cash, the history of dividend payments is logical. A company needs cash in order to pay dividends. You will discover that a consistent history of dividend payments goes hand in hand with long-term growth in the company's value and in the market value of its stock. The ability to pay dividends also depends on a company keeping its long-term debt under control. As more debt goes on the books, a growing amount of available cash flow has to be paid in interest to bondholders and other lenders, as well as repayments of principal. The higher the debt service, the less cash remains for dividends.

4. *Checking and comparing dividends is a great way to narrow a list of potential investments.* Some investors pick a short list of fundamental and technical criteria for stock selection. Even so, they

may end up with 20 or 30 companies they like. Most investors, for practical reasons, will do better narrowing their list to 10 or fewer companies. Checking the history of dividend payments and the current yield will help to pare down the list.

Investors tend to set goals for themselves. For example, they may decide to sell a stock if and when it gains 20 percent in value or doubles; they may also sell if and when the stock falls 10 percent or does not move at all. While many of these initial goals will be violated later based on changing conditions and perceptions, they are set on some basis.

It is a mistake to leave dividends out of this equation. For example, if you would like to experience a 10 percent appreciation per year, that is a difficult goal to reach. With the volatility in the market, few stocks have achieved consistent growth with reliability. Those that do rise 10 percent per year may also fall as much or more. Volatility equals risk. So as a consequence, it is often necessary to lower your goal somewhat. However, when you add dividends into the equation, goals are more easily reached. For example, if you would like to have annual appreciation of 10 percent on your original investment and a stock is paying a 3 percent dividend, you accomplish 30 percent of your goal just by purchasing the stock. Now you will reach your goal if the stock appreciates by 10 percent. And the fact that dividends can be reinvested in additional partial shares reduces your requirement even more. With compound dividends at play, each quarter's reinvestment grows slightly. For example, a $50 stock paying a 3 percent dividend grows by 3.03 percent per year with reinvested dividends:

Goal: Ten Percent Growth per Year	
Initial investment	$5,000.00
1st quarter dividend 3%, reinvested share balance	37.50
	$5,037.50
2nd quarter dividend 3%, reinvested share balance	37.78
	$5,075.28

3rd quarter dividend 3%, reinvested share balance	38.06
	$5,113.34
4th quarter dividend 3%, reinvested share balance	38.35
	$5,151.69
Compound return (151.69 ÷ 5,000)	3.03%

Now to reach a goal of 10 percent growth, you need the stock to grow by 6.97 percent (10.0 percent minus 3.03 percent):

Initial investment	$5,000.00
Dividend income	151.69
Capital gain, 6.97%	348.50
Total value	$5,500.19
Total return ($500.19 ÷ $5,000)	10.0%

To achieve this goal, you need the stock to rise only about $3^1/2$ points, or $350 on your investment of $5,000. Without dividends, you would need a five-point growth.

This illustration makes the point that dividends play a major role in overall profits on a stock portfolio, leading to conclusions that:

1. *It makes sense to pick stocks yielding better than average dividends.* Assuming that other fundamentals support the decision to purchase shares in a company, higher than average dividend yield is an attractive benefit. You will also discover that some of the best-managed companies also yield some of the best dividends—not always, but often.

2. *The overall goal-setting plan should be based on combined dividends and capital gains.* The dividend yield is going to be a major portion of overall return if stocks are picked wisely. It is quite easy to find stocks with a 3 percent, 4 percent, or 5 percent yield.

3. *Reinvesting dividends in additional partial shares helps reach goals in two ways.* By reinvesting dividends, you achieve a compound return on the dividends themselves. When you achieve

this by buying additional shares, you also benefit from any price appreciation, also on a compound basis.

Are dividends really that significant? How many highly rated stocks yield well? The following list (as of October 2007) includes stocks yielding above a 4 percent dividend, with a price-earnings (P/E) ratio under 20, and with earnings growth rating by Standard & Poor's (S&P) at 'A.' These criteria added together are an example of how you can narrow a selection list of stocks:[1]

Altria (MO)	4.23%
Citigroup (C)	4.93
U.S. Bancorp (USB)	4.98
Bank of America (BAC)	5.24
Wachovia (WB)	5.32
Fifth Third Bancorp (FITB)	5.51

This list includes financial stocks with one exception, Altria, but it makes the point that you can achieve 3 percent, 4 percent, or 5 percent returns on a portfolio just from dividend yield. The question of whether a particular industry is safe is yet another issue. For example, five of the six stocks in this list are financial, but is it safe to buy only financial stocks? Given the history of the 2007 market as an example, this sector had many problems related to the credit market and investments in housing but this only points out the danger of investing too heavily in any one industry. Diversification is essential, and additional industries include companies with high yields. For example, during the same period, utility company Consolidated Edison (ED) (5.03 percent dividend) and Abbott Labs (ABT) (5.03 percent) were also on the over-5 percent list. So you could include Washington Mutual (WM) (finance), Altria (MO) (tobacco), Consolidated Edison (utilities), and Abbott Labs (pharmaceutical) as four stocks in your portfolio. This is strongly diversified and yet the entire portfolio yielded over 5 percent.

This cannot be treated as a recommendation because it applied only to October 2007. But it demonstrates how selection based on dividend yield and other criteria can lead to some very handsome returns, with diversification and high yield at the same time.

Computing the Yield: Purchase Versus Current Value

Dividend yield (also called *current yield*) is an oddity, because it changes in a direction opposite the movement of stock. Companies declare dividends to be paid each year, usually once per quarter and expressed as a specific amount per share. For example, the company may declare that next year's dividend will be $1 per share. If you own 100 shares, you will get $100 per year in the form of a dividend, probably paid out at $25 per quarter.

To compute yield, divide the dollar amount of the dividend paid per year by the current price per share. This formula is shown in Figure 3-1.

For example, an annual dividend of $1 per share applies to a stock currently selling at $50 per share:

$$\frac{\$1}{\$50} = 2.0\%$$

The oddity of dividend calculations is seen in the way that yield changes when the stock price changes. Remember, the annual declaration remains unchanged for the year. In the example above, $1 per share is paid out at one-fourth the annual dividend, paid quarterly. But what happens if the price per share drops to $45? The dividend yield *rises* as a result:

FIGURE 3.1. DIVIDEND YIELD

$$\frac{\text{dividend per share}}{\text{price per share}} = \text{yield}$$

$$\frac{\$1}{\$45} = 2.2\%$$

The more the stock falls, the greater the yield. This raises a possibility for portfolio management based on the debate over whether you should buy more shares when prices fall. That suggestion observes that buying at an original price and then at a lower price reduces the overall cost of stock. If you buy 100 shares at $50 and another 100 at $45, your average cost per share is $47.50.

Some people suggest that you should not pay in more money when prices fall, but rather seek stock for which the market price is rising. However, if you bought shares at $50 per share, it has to be assumed that you considered that a good price (perhaps based on a combination of both P/E ratio and dividend, among other criteria). But as price falls, dividend yield rises and P/E falls, making the stock even more of a bargain at the lower price. As a strategy, well-selected stock at any given price based on sound selection criteria becomes a greater bargain if the price falls.

This is only true, of course, if no other fundamental realities have changed. For example, if a pharmaceutical company is being sued because its major drug proves to be dangerous, or if a company's product has to be withdrawn because it contains lead paint, then yesterday's fundamentals no longer apply. The test of a company's value is based not only on the financial ratios and trends, but also on the basic competitiveness of the company within the market.

As long as none of those market factors have changed, dividend yield is strategically important to you. Remember, the lower the price, the greater the dividend yield, because the dividend dollar value is fixed for the full year, even if the stock's price drops.

Does this mean the company is less valuable if the stock's price rises? Here again, there is a contradiction. The higher the price goes, the lower the dividend yield. If a $1 per share dividend is declared when the stock sells at $50 per share, it is a yield of 2 percent. But if the stock rises to $60 per share, the yield is reduced:

$$\frac{\$1}{\$60} = 1.7\%$$

Just as some people think you should buy more shares when stock prices fall, others believe you should buy more shares when prices rise. This *dollar-cost averaging* strategy usually calls for investing a fixed dollar amount every month, as an example. But when a stock's price rises, the consideration of dividend yield (and P/E) work adversely. Dividend yield is lowered but P/E rises as the stock's price rises. At such times, if you accept the lower current yield and higher P/E but still believe the stock is a bargain at that price, there is no reason to stay away. However, if you prefer higher yields and lower P/E ratios, you can seek other stocks whose price rise has not yet occurred.

Dividend History as a Crucial Test

Current yield is a useful test of a company's value, not only to reduce a list of potential investments but also to improve annual profits. Most people emphasize price change while ignoring dividend yield. If you set a profit goal, include dividends as part of that goal; you are likely to discover that dividends play a major part in the overall profitability of well-managed companies.

Looking beyond current yield, dividend history can provide further information for picking or eliminating companies as potential investments. You will find a rather large number of stocks yielding 3 percent, 4 percent, or 5 percent (or more) at any given time. If the total is well over 300 stocks, how do you eliminate these down to a more realistically sized list? Even if you seek highest-rated stocks and look only in a specified P/E range, the list remains large. As of October 2007, the number of stocks yielding more than 4 percent, rated with the high credit risk of 'A' and with P/E under 20, exceeded 70 stocks.[2]

Another way to use dividends to pare down the list is to check the history of dividend growth over several years. Mergent Company publishes a quarterly summary of its "Dividend Achievers," stocks whose dividends have increased over 10 years or more. These stocks have consistently outperformed market-wide indices like the S&P 500, and by mid-2007, 312 companies met this impor-

tant standard. That is about 10 percent of North American companies that pay dividends to stockholders. The company's Web site, at
http://www.dividendachievers.com, reported that nearly half of the
companies on its 2007 list had actually seen annual dividend growth
over more than 20 years, and that 98.5 percent of the companies on
the list were profitable with lower volatility than typical stocks.

In other words, these dividend achievers represent one important method for reducing the list of potential stocks. But why is this
so? A company that is able to increase its dividend every year over
10 to 20 years has adequate cash flow to be able to make payments
to its stockholders. In comparison, companies having cash flow dif-
ficulties cannot pay ever-higher dividends due to cash shortages. So
you can analyze cash flow with a series of financial ratios over time,
or you can simply study the dividend history of a company to decide
whether management is doing a good job. It is accurate to assume
that when a company increases its annual dividend, management is
better than average.

The four companies previously mentioned, all yielding over 5
percent dividend, all met the 10-year dividend achiever test through
fiscal 2006. Your criteria for low to medium P/E, high credit rating,
and high dividend could be further narrowed by looking only for
dividend achievers. Table 3-1 shows the 10-year history for the four
stocks used in the previous high-dividend example.

Accompanying the test of dividends is a question related to
overall capitalization. Check the dividends, but also keep an eye on
the debt ratio (more on this in the next section). There is a natural
conflict between stockholders (equity investors) and bondholders
or lenders (debt investors). The two together provide capitalization
to the company and each gets a slice of the pie. Stockholders get
price appreciation in a well-managed company as well as dividends
if and when these are paid. Debt investors get interest on money
loaned. Bondholders are usually paid before common stock owners
in the event of liquidation. So if the company goes broke and sells
off everything, a debt investor has an advantage over an equity investor. But as long as your company remains in business and is well
managed and competitive, price appreciation is a major benefit of
owning stock.

TABLE 3-1. HIGH-YIELDING DIVIDEND ACHIEVER STOCKS

Year	Consolidated Edison	Dividend per Share Abbott Labs	Altria	Washington Mutual
2006	$2.30	$1.16	$3.32	$2.06
2005	2.28	1.09	3.06	1.90
2004	2.26	1.03	2.82	1.74
2003	2.24	0.97	2.64	1.40
2002	2.22	0.92	2.44	1.06
2001	$2.20	$0.82	$2.22	$0.90
2000	2.18	0.74	2.02	0.76
1999	2.14	0.66	1.80	0.65
1998	2.12	0.58	1.64	0.55
1997	2.10	0.52	1.60	0.47

Source: Standard & Poor's Stock Reports

When price appreciation is combined with a healthy dividend, you are in the best position of all. But a hidden danger is the creeping long-term debt. If debt begins to rise over time, the company could be headed for trouble. The higher the debt, the greater the "debt service" (requirement to repay the amount borrowed, plus interest). And the higher the debt service, the less working capital remains for dividend payments. If the debt level exceeds the company's rate of growth, dividends will stop growing as well.

Dividends Versus Interest: Total Capitalization

Total capitalization is one of the most important features to be aware of. It represents the overall source of capitalization for the business and contains two segments. First is the value of net worth, also called stockholders' equity. This is the combination of capital stock and retained earnings (the net of all profits or losses). The equity portion of total capitalization is only part of the story, however. The rest is debt capitalization, which is identified on the balance sheet as long-term debt. This includes long-term notes, contracts payable (business loans, mortgages, etc.), and bonds. The level of debt can be quite low or very substantial. Some companies carry little or no debt, whereas a few have very high debt. General Motors, for example, reported that debt represented 115 percent of total capitalization at the end of 2006, an extreme case. This means that the equity portion was *negative*. In GM's case, it was more than $5.4 billion in the red.

Total capitalization is a critical test of how well companies manage their cash, and how heavily they depend on debt versus equity. The formula for total capitalization is summarized in Figure 3-2.

For example, if long-term debt (in millions of dollars) is $2,714 and total equity is $1,388, total capitalization will be $4,102:

$$\$2,714 + \$1,388 = \$4,102$$

To compute the all-important debt ratio, divide long-term debt by total capitalization. This ratio, expressed as a percentage, shows current status as well as the trend in debt levels. It is summarized in Figure 3-3.

FIGURE 3.2. TOTAL CAPITALIZATION

long-term debt + total equity = total capitalization

FIGURE 3.3. DEBT RATIO

$$\frac{\text{long-term debt}}{\text{total capitalization}} = \text{debt ratio}$$

For example, if long-term debt (in millions of dollars) is $2,714 and total capitalization is $4,102, the debt ratio is 66.2 percent:

$$\frac{\$2,714}{\$4,102} = 66.2\%$$

Additional typical examples and comparisons are summarized in Table 3-2.

In this comparison, dissimilar years are reported because fiscal years end in different months. But in each case, these are the latest available results as of fall 2007. Note the vast differences among these three companies. Microsoft (MSFT) carries virtually no debt, so its working capital risk is practically zero. In comparison, Wal-Mart (WMT) carries a consistent debt equal to about one-third of

TABLE 3-2. DEBT RATIO AND TOTAL CAPITALIZATION

		In Millions of Dollars		
		Long-Term	Total	Debt
Company	Year	Debt	Capitalization	Ratio
Microsoft	2007	$ 0	$31,097	0%
	2006	0	40,104	0
	2005	0	48,115	0
	2004	0	74,825	0
	2003	0	62,751	0
Wal-Mart	2007	$30,735	$94,468	32.5%
	2006	30,171	84,809	35.6
	2005	23,669	74,388	31.8
	2004	20,099	65,206	30.8
	2003	19,608	60,307	32.5
Eastman Kodak	2006	$ 2,714	$ 4,102	66.2%
	2005	2,764	4,731	58.4
	2004	1,852	5,663	32.7
	2003	2,322	5,566	41.4
	2002	1,164	3,941	29.5

Source: Standard & Poor's Stock Reports

total capitalization, and this trend has not changed over a five-year period even though the company experienced considerable growth. Eastman Kodak (EK), however, has experienced a rising debt ratio. In fiscal 2002, debt was only 29.5 percent of total capitalization, but at the end of 2006 it had more than doubled to 66.2 percent.

Dividend declarations may change for a variety of reasons. But it is interesting to note that the dividend trend for these three companies was related to the trend in the debt ratio. Table 3-3 summarizes the dividend history for the same period.

Microsoft and Wal-Mart both increased their dividends for each year reported, in line with increasing revenues and profits. However, Microsoft also carries no debt and Wal-Mart was able to contain its debt to the same level while its markets grew. Kodak's story

TABLE 3-3. DEBT RATIO AND DIVIDENDS

Company	Year	Debt Ratio	Dividend per Share
Microsoft	2007	0%	$0.39
	2006	0	0.34
	2005	0	0.32*
	2004	0	0.16
	2003	0	0.08
Wal-Mart	2007	32.5%	$0.67
	2006	35.6	0.60
	2005	31.8	0.52
	2004	30.8	0.36
	2003	32.5	0.30
Eastman Kodak	2006	66.2%	$0.50
	2005	58.4	0.50
	2004	32.7	0.50
	2003	41.4	1.15
	2002	29.5	1.80

* Microsoft's reported dividend excludes a one-time $3.00 per share dividend

Source: Standard & Poor's Stock Reports

was not as successful. Its overall dividend declined from $1.80 to $0.50 per share over the period, and for the past three years the dividend remained at the same level without any growth. In fact, given the rise in the debt ratio, even that level of dividend payment seems unjustified.

Dividend and debt ratio history are revealing when analyzed together. The situation often reflects the trend in profits as well. For example, during this period both Microsoft and Wal-Mart reported strong growth in profits, but Kodak reported diminishing profits each year (in millions of dollars):

Year	Profit (loss)
2006	(600)
2005	(1,455)
2004	81
2003	238
2002	793

It makes sense. A company that is losing money as its market share declines (or, in the case of Kodak, when its primary product is becoming obsolete as in the case of old-style film for cameras), it is impossible to continue increasing dividends every year. The companies that are able to reflect growth in dividends per share while keeping long-term debt in check are effectively managing cash flow, remaining competitive, and rewarding stockholders with not only dividends, but with ever-higher stock prices as well.

Calculating *Total* Return: Capital Gains Plus Dividends

The inclusion of dividends as part of overall return is necessary if you expect to make realistic comparisons between stocks. Some companies pay exceptionally high dividends, including those above 5 percent; others pay very low dividends or none at all. Some very large corporations pay dividends at quite a low rate as of 2007, including Exxon-Mobil (XOM) (1.5 percent), IBM (1.4 percent), Microsoft (1.5 percent), Target (TGT) (0.95 percent), and Wal-Mart (1.95 percent). Xerox Corporation (XRX) pays no dividends. If you want to compare these companies to those yielding above 5 percent, you need to include dividend yield.

The basic calculation of return from investment in stock is to divide the profit by the original net cost (price paid plus transaction fees including margin interest, if applicable). Figure 3-4 shows this calculation.

For example, if you bought 100 shares of stock at $50 per share and paid $5,012 (including transaction costs) and later sold the stock at $56 per share, receiving $5,588, your return is:

$$\frac{\$5,588 - \$5,012}{\$5,012} = 11.5\%$$

The profit of $576 represents 11.5 percent, but by itself, this is meaningless. For example, if you achieved an 11.5 percent return on two stocks, they would be vastly different if your holding period was not identical. In order to make *valid* comparisons between investments, you need to annualize the returns. This means adjusting the return to what it would have been if the holding period was exactly one year.

To annualize, divide the return by the holding period (in months) and then multiply by 12 (months). This formula is shown in Figure 3-5.

FIGURE 3.4. PROFIT FROM SALE OF STOCK

$$\frac{\text{sales price} - \text{purchase price}}{\text{purchase price}} = \text{profit}$$

FIGURE 3.5. ANNUALIZED RETURN

$$\left(\frac{\text{return}}{\text{holding period}} \right) \quad \times \quad 12 \quad = \text{ annualized return}$$

For example, the 11.5 percent return will be vastly different if the holding period is shorter or longer than one year:

Three-Month Holding Period

$$(11.5\% \div 3) \times 12 = 46.0\%$$

Fifteen-Month Holding Period

$$(11.5\% \div 15) \times 12 = 9.2\%$$

The longer the holding period, the lower the annualized yield. The difference in this example between 3 and 15 months is vast. It is essential to go through the annualization to make sure you are making like-kind comparisons.

Dividends have to be included in the calculation, but you do not need to annualize the rate of dividend return. This is especially complex if you reinvest dividend income in additional partial shares. If you begin with the calculation based on total dollar value and then annualize total capital gain and dividend together, you get a fairly accurate picture. Dividend income does not distort the total.

However, it remains important to include dividend income. For example, if your 100-share investment was made in two identically priced stocks at the same time, will total return calculations be the same? If one stock paid 5.25 percent and the other paid no dividend, a 12-month holding period outcome would be quite different:

Stock Paying 5.25% Dividend

100 shares sold after 12-month holding period	
less original cost	$5,588
	−5,012
capital gain	$ 576
dividend, 5.25% at purchase value $5,012	263
total return	$ 839
total yield ($839 ÷ $5,012)	16.7%

Stock Paying No Dividend

100 shares sold after 12-month holding period	$5,588
less original cost	−5,012
capital gain and total return	$ 576
total yield ($576 ÷ $5,012)	11.5%

This demonstrates the significance of dividend yield. The capital gains on stock sales may be marginal in percentage terms. For example, a $250 profit on a $5,000 investment is only a 5 percent return without considering annualization. If that stock yielded a 5.25 percent dividend, then you earned more from dividends than from sale of stock.

Calculating yield is not difficult. It is a key indicator for a stock, especially when looked at in a historical context. Making realistic calculations of actual outcome with annualization in mind affects comparisons as well; clearly, a return on holdings of a few months is not the same as one for stock held for more than a full year.

Yield is one way to judge value and to make value judgments about stocks. Another way is to review the past in order to predict the future of price movement, hoping to find stocks with the greatest potential for price appreciation. Managing risk is a balancing act between this profit opportunity and market volatility. In the next chapter, the well-known Dow Theory is explained in a different context than its familiar application. It is usually applied to the whole market, but its principles can also be valuable in analyzing individual stocks.

▓ Notes

1 Source: Charles Schwab & Co. brokerage Web site at *https://investing.schwab.com.*
2 *Ibid.*

THE "PRACTICAL" DOW THEORY

A lot of emphasis is placed on the Dow Jones Industrial Average (DJIA), an index of 30 large-cap companies. However, in spite of the popular belief, the Dow is not "the market," only a sample of stocks. While the DJIA is widely followed and believed to indicate what is going on in the market, it is not always true, especially when it comes to a study of the value in each and every stock. There are two considerations: trends in the broad market that are found in the indices, and trends in the individual company that are found in movement of its stock price.

The origin of the Dow Theory is traced back to the founder of the Dow Jones Company and publisher of what has become the *Wall Street Journal*, Charles Dow. However, Dow developed his ideas as a method for studying business trends, that is, sales and earnings. Today, the same theory is invariably applied to the broader market as defined by the DJIA. Because it is general in nature, it tells the investor absolutely nothing about whether the timing is right to buy, sell, or hold a specific stock.

This chapter shows how the principles of the Dow Theory can

be applied with effectiveness to individual stocks held in a portfolio. The cornerstone ideas of identifying primary movements and confirming them separately works well for individual stocks, but such an approach is rarely used. Among the means for identifying such trends in stocks, the all-important subjects explained in the first two chapters work as essential elements in the study of a stock's trend.

As the basis for the very premise of technical analysis, the Dow Theory can be useful in employing technical tests: trading range, price volatility, and support/resistance.

How Indexing Works: Weighted Averages

The Dow Jones Industrial Average is just that, an *average* of price movement among 30 industrial stocks. Collectively, these 30 stocks represent nearly 24 percent of the overall market capitalization of U.S.-based publicly listed companies, making the index a strong indicator of the U.S. economy and business climate.[1]

The DJIA is a weighted average, meaning that as companies on the list grow and split their stock, the weighting changes. Over time, those stocks with higher share prices carry a higher weighting factor than stocks whose share price is smaller. The DJIA is called a *price-weighted index* because expensive shares have more influence on the trend than cheaper shares. Ironically, this has nothing to do with actual capitalization. The share price is merely the current market value per share. Does this mean that a company with a $100 stock is "better" than one with an $80 stock? No. If the $100 stock's company has 5 million shares, total capital value is $500 million. If the company with the $80 stock has 10 million shares outstanding, its total capital value is $800 million.

The disparity created by a price-weighted index is considerable. For every point of influence a $100 stock has on movement of the DJIA, an $80 stock has only 0.8 points of weighting and a $50 stock has only 0.5 points.

Some indices are market value–weighted, a system much different than the DJIA. In these indices, the value of each component stock is weighted based on total capital. Returning to the previous example, a $100 stock whose company has $500 million in capital would be much different than an $80 stock with $800 million in capital. For every point of weighting in the $800 million company, the $500 million company would carry five-eighths the point value in the index.

The impact of a price change is where this makes a difference. In a price-weighted stock, the higher-priced issues will have correspondingly greater influence on movement of the average. In a capital value–weighted index, influence depends on the overall value of the company.

Some well-known market value–weighted indices include the NASDAQ Composite Index, the NYSE Composite Index, and the S&P 500. The S&P 500 has modified its weighted method and is not "float-weighted." This means that only shares available for public trading are counted in the weighting. This is a subtle distinction, but the problem of market analysis remains: Daily financial news programs like to report on movement in the DJIA, the NASDAQ, and the S&P. But in fact, these three indices are all computed in different ways: price-weighted, market-weighted, and float-weighted.

Most people continue to judge the market by the DJIA. Without any doubt, current trends and strength or weakness in this widely followed index are good indicators of overall market conditions. The distinctions between bull and bear markets are defined largely by how the DJIA moves or fails to move. A summary of the 30 stocks in the DJIA and their weighting as of late February 2008 is provided in Table 4-1.

The higher-priced stocks on the DJIA have the greatest influence, as this table reveals. At the time of these weighting factors (October 2007), five stocks [3M (MMM), Boeing, (BA), Chevron (CVX), Exxon-Mobil, and IBM] held over 29 percent of the total weighting of the DJIA. This is significant. These higher-priced stocks and their fortunes on the market may actually distort the conditions in the broader market for some relatively isolated events. For example, say that Exxon-Mobil's stock rose many points following the rising price of oil, and at the same time Boeing received new contracts for dozens of planes while IBM and 3M also reached new agreements expanding their market share. It is conceivable that the DJIA could rise significantly even if other components were weak

TABLE 4-1. DOW JONES INDUSTRIAL AVERAGE COMPONENTS

Company	Weighting %	Company	Weighting %
3M	5.16%	Hewlett-Packard	3.14%
Alcoa	2.50	Home Depot	1.86
American Express	2.96	Intel	1.33
AIG	3.35	IBM	7.47
AT&T	2.26	Johnson & Johnson	4.04
Bank of America	2.75%	JPMorgan Chase	2.85%
Boeing	5.38	McDonalds	3.55
Caterpillar	4.76	Merck	2.92
Chevron	5.66	Microsoft	1.81
Citigroup	1.65	Pfizer	1.46
Coca-Cola	3.85%	Proctor & Gamble	4.31%
E.I. DuPont	3.05	United Technologies	4.68
Exxon-Mobil	5.73	Verizon	2.33
General Electric	2.18	Wal-Mart	3.30
General Motors	1.59	Walt Disney	2.12
		Total	100.00%

Source: Dow Jones & Co., as of February 26, 2007 rounded down

and the overall market were in poor condition. The likelihood of such distortions occurring chronically is small. These companies are in different industries and are internationally diversified, so economic impacts of any significance are likely to be mirrored among the entire market, but the issue is worth being aware of. The 30 industrials carry a lot of influence through the DJIA, and relatively few companies in the 30—four, in fact—account for nearly one-fourth of the total DJIA movement.

The History of the Dow Theory

It is interesting to trace back and see where the DJIA came from, and how it has become such an influential market indicator today.

The origin goes back more than 125 years to 1882 when Charles Dow and his partner, Edward Jones, formed Dow Jones & Company.

In 1880, Charles Dow, a 29-year-old business writer with only a limited formal education, arrived in New York after working for several years as a financial writer in Providence, Rhode Island. While in Rhode Island, Dow met fellow financial writer Edward Jones when the two worked together at the *Providence Evening Press*. Dow was asked by his New York employer to recommend a second reporter; thus Dow brought Jones into the Kiernan Wall Street Financial News Bureau. Two years later Dow and Jones started their famous financial organization, originally located in the basement of a candy store. A year after that, they began publishing the *Customers' Afternoon Letter*, a two-page summary of each day's important financial news and reports. They also devised an index called the Dow Jones Stock Average, which included 11 companies (nine railroads, one steamship company, and Western Union). On July 8, 1889, the two-page report evolved into the first edition of *The Wall Street Journal* (originally available for two cents per issue).

One of the big problems in those days, many years before federal regulation, was a tendency for companies to pay for favorable press stories. Dow forbade his reporters from the practice of exchanging favorable stories for stock tips and began a new procedure: publishing the names of companies that refused to provide profit and loss information for publication. These high ethical standards quickly earned the new paper a great deal of respect and a lot of power and influence on Wall Street.

On May 26, 1896, Dow published a new average of 12 stocks. Dow simply added their prices together and then divided by 12 (to arrive at the average). The following year the paper added a railroad average. Most important among Dow's innovations was his development of what is today called the Dow Theory. Dow saw a clear relationship between trends in stock prices and other business trends. He thought that whenever his industrial and railroad averages were moving in the same direction, it was a significant sign.

Dow did not envision applying this trend analysis to the overall market, at least not as a primary way of judging stocks. His observations were based on analysis of corporate internal trends in revenues, costs, expenses, and profits and how those trends translated to changes in stock prices. He also noted that stocks tended to move in predictable cycles tied to economic and industrial trends, which also were reflected in market activity. Dow's original concept found application in internal business practices. It was only after his death that Dow Jones & Company began applying Dow's original observations to market-wide trends. They developed the Dow Theory by formalizing a series of observations originally noted by Dow himself.

The averages produced by Dow provided market observers with a methodology for deciding whether a market trend was up or down. By combining stocks together into a single index, the direction and strength were easily implied. Dow further believed that industrial and railroad average trends could serve to confirm an evolving direction within the market. By 1896, the railroad average (renamed the transportation average in 1970) was increased to 20 stocks and many years later, in 1929, the company added the utility average.

In 1926, the size of the industrial average was increased to 30 issues, where it has remained ever since. That same year, the method of calculation was adjusted to avoid distortions when companies split their stocks, which ultimately led to today's price-weighted method. Today, the DJIA is the most widely cited index, and in most circles it is considered the primary measurement of market strength or weakness.

The term "Dow Theory" was first used by S.A. Nelson in his 1903 book, *The ABC of Stock Speculation*. In his book (he refers to "Dow's Theory" and devotes 15 chapters to the concept), Nelson summarizes Dow's writings into a cogent single theory that could be applied against the entire market to spot trends and judge current conditions. Using Dow's editorials from the preceding 20 years, Nelson created a technical market theory that dominates the market today.

In fact, the Dow Theory has survived through more than 100 years of change. As one writer observed in 1963,

Dow's basic principles have continued to function effectively in the more than 60 years since his death and throughout a period which has encompassed both the horse-and-buggy and the space ages; two world wars; the ascendancy of communism throughout the world; the vast changes in political, social, and economic philosophies both at home and abroad . . .[2]

Guiding Principles: Major Trends and Confirmations

The Dow Theory determines whether markets can be defined as optimistic and up-trending (bull market) or pessimistic and downtrending (bear market). The theory as it is applied today contains six specific tenets, or rules:

1. *Markets contain three trends.* The three trends are well known. An *uptrend* occurs when two things take place. Prices close at a higher level than before while low price levels in the same period are higher with each rally (higher highs and higher lows). A *downtrend* is characterized by lower-closing low prices offset by lower high prices in each subsequent rally (lower lows and lower highs). The third trend involves a clear direction and then a period of price movement in the opposite direction, ending with a return to the established trend.

2. *Trends contain three distinct phases.* The Dow Theory also divides a trend into three segments. First is the *accumulation* phase, in which knowledgeable investors buy (in an uptrend) or sell (in a downtrend), often when the market-wide opinion is in the opposite direction. Second is the *public participation* phase, in which a larger segment of investors recognizes the trend and follows it, often leading to higher volume and speculation. (The "crowd" usually follows the trend, buying at or near the high and selling at or near the low.) Third is the *distribution* phase, in which wise investors distribute their shares to the market (selling long positions or buying to close shorts).

3. *All news and information is discounted by the stock market.* Market prices are believed to absorb all news quite rapidly, even in anticipation of what has not yet been announced. For example, if an earnings report is due on Friday and most people think it will beat analysts' estimates, then on Wednesday and Thursday prices are likely to rise in anticipation of the good news. Bad news is similarly taken into the price and discounted in the current price levels and trends. This "efficiency" is assumed and has been expanded into the "efficient market hypothesis" (see the next section for more about this).

4. *Market averages must confirm one another before a new trend can be called.* Dow believed that railroads were essential to economic conditions because goods had to be shipped from manufacturer to market. This interdependency meant that industrial growth had to be accompanied by a similar pattern in the rails (transportation stocks). This logical observation led to the theory of confirmation. When two averages begin moving in the same direction, it signals a new trend; once one of those averages begins to diverge, it anticipates a change in the trend.

5. *Price trends are confirmed by volume of trading.* When price change happens on low trading volume, it could be caused by any number of external forces, such as short covering or takeover rumors. But whenever price change is accompanied by high volume, it serves as further confirmation that the trend is real.

6. *Trends continue until subsequent signals prove that they have ended and new trends have begun.* This is perhaps the most important of the Dow Theory tenets. From day to day, it is very difficult to read the trend because prices move up and down, often in very volatile change patterns. A trend is not actually ended and reversed until the signals are there to confirm (phase changes, confirmation, and volume).

Not everyone agrees with or accepts the Dow Theory as the last word. It has always been controversial and, like all theories, it is not perfect. Depending on the time period studied, the Dow Theory may beat the more traditional "buy-and-hold" approach so popular among value investors (that is, find bargain-priced stocks for exceptionally well-managed companies, then buy and hold for the long term). A study published in 1933 concluded that buy and hold produced a 15.5 percent return versus the Dow Theory strategy's 12 percent, during the period 1902–1929.[3]

That study was also controversial and possibly inaccurate. The absolute returns of the buy-and-hold approach cannot be compared to the risk-adjusted returns possible by moving in and out of issues based on Dow Theory indicators. Market timing strategies may be higher risk but may produce potentially greater rates of return. The only reasonable conclusion is that any theory is going to work well in times when the trends play out according to what the theory anticipates, and when that does not happen, the same theory appears less reliable. The Dow Theory is not the only technical approach, however. Two additional ideas also find their own followers. These are the random walk theory and the efficient market hypothesis.

Even with its controversial interpretations, the Dow Theory is fascinating and useful in judging market conditions. Without indices and methods for taking the stock market's temperature, investors would never know where matters stand. If you listen to economic data published by the government, you know that economic indicators are often contradictory or have little immediate impact on stock market conditions; so relying on these data is not satisfactory for most people. The Dow Theory and indices like the DJIA, the S&P 500, and the NASDAQ all help to place a conditional value on the market at any given moment in the day, or within a larger, longer-term trend.

Alternative Technical Theories

The Dow Theory has certainly stood the test of time. Given the incredible changes in technology during the past century, this is quite amazing. In the days when Charles Dow was writing his essays concerning business trends, there were no airplanes, freeways, or computers. Most people lived on farms and never traveled more than 20 miles from their places of birth. Only insiders were able to participate in markets for the most part, and anyone who wanted to invest had to rely on brokers, whose activities were not regulated by either federal or state governments.

However, the Dow Theory is not the sole technical approach to the stock market. It does establish a methodical process for making consistent judgments about whether the overall economic mood is positive or negative, but some market observers contend that this approach is not the only way to look at the market. Two additional beliefs, the random walk theory and the efficient market hypothesis, should be considered as well.

The *random walk theory* contends that it is impossible to predict market movements. Academic tests involving picking stocks with coin flips appear to support the idea that there is a 50/50 chance of a stock's rising or falling, but this ignores the qualifying *reasons* for such changes. Of course there is a 50/50 chance of movement, and there are only two directions possible other than a no-change outcome. But both technical and fundamental reasons have much more to do with how stock prices change than actual randomness. If you try to apply the random walk theory to any other supply-and-demand market, its flaws become obvious very quickly.

For example, what if someone told you that there was a 50/50 chance that housing prices would rise or fall? Historically, housing prices in robust economic markets rise over time. By "robust," this means strong job growth, moderate to low crime levels, and other desirable attributes. As long as jobs are growing and people are safe, housing values will rise. More people want to move to nice areas, which places pressure on prices. Supply and demand is an obvious force economically speaking, so housing prices rise. People need a place to live, and as they can afford to buy homes rather than renting, this theory makes sense in many ways. There may be such phenomena as housing bubbles, overpricing, and actual declines in value in some areas, but in most situations housing values rise predictably. There is nothing random about it.

The argument using the housing market makes sense, especially when you recognize that predictability of future value is a factor of clearly understood economic drivers: jobs, tax benefits, climate, quality of life, crime levels, ease of commute, and social and recreational outlets. The attributes that cause housing prices to rise consistently over time are sensible and widely understood.

The same concept applies to the stock market, disputing the random walk theory in virtually every case. As an academic theory, it is interesting and worthy of discussion but it simply does not work out. Consider the comparisons between stocks with technical and fundamental attributes as summarized in Table 4-2.

The differences between stocks with these basic attributes are glaring. It is not only reasonable to assume that these attributes determine future price direction; it is inevitable. Stocks with strong technical and fundamental outcomes do increase in value, just as

TABLE 4-2. STOCK COMPARISONS

Positive Attributes	Negative Attributes
Technical Analysis:	
narrow trading range moves upward over time	volatile trading range with unpredictable direction or trend
gradual price growth over many years	gradual price decline over many years
P/E ratio between 10 and 25	P/E ratio between 60 and 110
Fundamental Analysis:	
current ratio of 2 to 1	current ratio of 1 to 3
debt ratio between zero and 25% and remaining the same over many years	debt ratio between 50% and 75% and increasing each year
dividend above 4%	dividend between zero and 1%
dividend has increased every year for 10 years or more	dividend has not increased or some dividends have been skipped
sales and earnings increase every year	sales grow but earnings fall
net earnings and core earnings are close together with only minor adjustments	big adjustments occur every year between net and core earnings

those with deteriorating attributes tend to reflect a negative price trend. The random walk theory is an interesting academic exercise, but it is easily disputed.

The *efficient market hypothesis* is an outgrowth of the Dow Theory, which observes that all news is discounted in the current price. In fact, the concept that the market is efficient supports the random walk theory in some respects. If the market were efficient, meaning that the current price reflects all known news and information, then future price movement might be truly random. But like the random walk theory, the efficient market hypothesis is clearly flawed and false.

In fact, the market is highly inefficient. You consistently see price changes overreacting to news and information as it is released. When analysts estimate earnings of $5.02 per share and actual earnings come in at $5.01, the stock may fall several points. It does not matter that the earnings are the best ever, or that the company making the report is very pleased with the outcome. All that matters is that the report was "disappointing" because it was one penny per share lower than the estimates. This is unrealistic.

By the same argument, stocks may increase unreasonably. In 2007, Microsoft stock rose by five points, or about 12 percent, in one day (October 26) following $4.3 billion net income in the latest quarter versus $3.5 billion the year before. Microsoft is an excellent company with nice profit margins and no long-term debt, but it is extremely unusual for a large-cap company to experience a one-day spike in stock price above 10 percent. This is a case of the market overreacting to news. Even though it was good news, the jump in price is an oddity. Such momentary changes, usually followed by corrections later the same day or the next day, are not at all uncommon.

The market is anything but efficient. It overreacts to virtually all changes, positive and negative. The fluctuations in price from moment to moment reflect ever-moving interaction between buyers and sellers, short-selling and covering of positions, poorly timed long positions being opened and closed, and self-serving timing decisions by large mutual funds. None of these market forces are by any means efficient. Anyone with money in the market knows—

often painfully—that the efficient market hypothesis is an interesting theory but far from practical.

Both random walk theory and efficient market hypothesis are popular beliefs in academic circles, because they are comforting to those who choose to believe in them. Most of the people who subscribe to these beliefs do not have real money at risk in the market, however, but function in the academic world only. This is a harsh indictment of both technical beliefs; however, they do serve a purpose. The proposition that the market and its pricing is somehow out of the hands of investors raises issues worthy of discussion. This leads to greater diligence in identifying the technical and fundamental attributes of stocks that make it possible to pick stocks in a nonrandom manner, and to cope with the inherent inefficiency of the market. In fact, the nonrandom nature of the market points the way to picking stocks well, and the inefficiency (even irrationality) also provides profit opportunities. Because the market is ruled by emotions such as greed and fear, those who keep a cooler head and are able to work against a crowd mentality are likely to time their decisions better than the average investor.

This idea—buying when most people are in a panic and selling, or selling when everyone else is in a euphoric state of greed and buying—is called *contrarian* investing. Many people have noticed that there is a tendency to "buy high and sell low" instead of the other way around. The "crowd" operates on greed and fear, and that means that a contrarian can go against the flow, and rather than following the crowd, makes contrary decisions. This means selling when the "conventional wisdom" says "buy, buy, buy" and buying when everyone else is in a panic and believes that the market is about to crash.

Contrarians are more likely to profit in the market because they take profits at or near the top and buy bargains at or near the bottom. The success of the contrarian approach demonstrates the false premise of both random walk theory and efficient market hypothesis. It is a philosophy of investing that observes a fact: "Bulls and bears can both make a profit in the market, but pigs and chickens cannot."

The Problem for Portfolio Analysis: Applying Technical Theories

Many technical theories are based on broad index analysis. This is why the DJIA is such a popular indicator. It tells you whether the market is up or down. But when it comes to individual stocks, does the DJIA actually help?

Application of any index is going to be broad, so it can only provide you with a general indicator of the market's health at the moment. When it comes to picking stocks, you need some stock-specific indicators, whether technical or fundamental.

Many stocks follow index direction, so it would be unrealistic to discount the value of the DJIA, the S&P 500, and the NASDAQ. They provide valuable insights and are fine as starting points. Obviously, people are more likely to want to get into the market when the direction is upward, when enthusiasm is visible, and when prices are rising across a broad spectrum. But picking a specific stock requires the use of more directed tests. The decision to buy, hold, or sell a specific stock cannot be tied to the DJIA.

As Charles Dow observed more than a century ago, trends mean something. If you see a trend in an individual stock, it is there for a reason. There is nothing magical or mysterious about how or why prices change; the reasons can always be found and once you see how the cause and effect works, it becomes easier to make market decisions in the future. By the time a trend turns and begins moving in the opposite direction, it is too late to make decisions. It is critical to develop a system for studying stock trends that *anticipates* what is going to happen. Timing a buy or sell decision based on trends as they occur is a far more sensible and profitable system than trying to react *after* a trend has ended. Hindsight is valuable, but it rarely leads to profits.

Making predictions is always elusive, but good predictions are possible, especially concerning high-quality stocks in well-managed companies. For example, Microsoft is clearly a leader in its industry. The stock has a history of trading in a narrow range but moving relentlessly upward over many years. The company carries no debt and it produces a high-quality product. They have had their share of problems, but sector leaders are always big targets for competitors. Microsoft has been sued endlessly over its entire history, but the product quality is indisputable and the stock's history proves one basic truth about the market: Well-managed companies reward their stockholders.

The same observation works in the opposite direction. General Motors, one of the best examples of a company that has literally been run into the ground over several decades, reported growing revenues with shrinking net profits, and massive core earnings adjustments. Its debt is greater than 100 percent of equity capitalization. Its pension liabilities (which don't show up on the balance sheet) are *higher* than the company's total net worth. And, not surprisingly, the stock price has fallen drastically over many years. In 1997, GM stock traded between $72 and $52 per share. In 2006, it traded between $37 and $18. The reason: ever-falling net profits and rising debt, and perhaps most importantly of all, a declining profitability ratio. Revenues rose every year in that decade, while profits plummeted.

There is nothing random in the GM fundamental or technical history, and the same can be said about Microsoft. They are good examples of how poorly managed companies fail to compete in a global market (GM versus Honda [HMC] and Toyota [TM], for example), and how well-managed companies only get better over time (Microsoft as a global leader in its industry, for example).

Realistically, you need to study and understand the various market theories and then simply place them in perspective. The Dow Theory has stood the test of time even in a rapidly changing world because it makes sense and has been proven useful in understanding the stock market. The random walk theory and efficient market hypothesis are interesting concepts for discussion, but only to the extent that they demonstrate the importance of analysis, both technical and fundamental. These two theories are cynical because they imply that as investors, people have no way of controlling their own destinies. Both theories tell you that the market is random and completely chance, or that prices are so efficient that you can never find bargains. These beliefs are false and the real truth—that you can find quality investments through analysis and study—is far more reassuring.

Applying the Dow Theory to Individual Stocks

The problem with the Dow Theory as it is used today is that it is usually considered a market-wide indicator. It provides no guidance in the timing of buy and sell decisions for individual stocks. However, the precepts in the Dow Theory can be used to help make decisions in a timely manner for each stock.

No stock is going to follow the broader market exactly, so you can apply Dow Theory tenets to individual stocks and gain insight. It is a useful exercise to review each of the six observations in the Dow Theory as they can be applied to buying and selling individual stocks rather than judging the direction of the overall market. The six points:

1. *Markets contain three trends.* The uptrend, downtrend, and temporary reversal trend apply to all market-wide movements. They also apply to specific stocks. In fact, for traders who want to move in and out of stocks in the short term rather than holding shares for many years, observation of trends is a valuable method for timing buy and sell moves. Day traders (those who move in and out of positions within a single trading day) and swing traders (those who complete transactions usually within three to five days) use these trends as their primary tools. Under swing trading definitions, any trend of three or more changes creates a setup. An uptrend consists of three or more consecutive periods in which each subsequent trading range has higher highs offset by higher lows. A downtrend consists of three or more consecutive periods in which each subsequent trading range has lower lows offset by lower highs. A setup is found when these trends end. After three or more downward movements, a "buy" is signaled. After three or more upward movements, a "sell" is signaled.

2. *Trends contain three distinct phases.* Accumulation, public participation, and distribution apply to specific stocks as well as to

overall markets. Wise investors accumulate positions before the market crowd does so. Public participation happens once the "crowd" recognizes the trend and gets in. Distribution is when the positions are closed at the end of the trend. The classic contrarian sequences involve buying shares when the stock is out of favor (accumulation), enjoying the benefits of the price being driven up when the crowd enters the stock (public participation), and selling at or near the high and in advance of a reversal (distribution). The same sequence can be applied by short sellers in the sequence of sell, hold, and buy to close.

3. *All news and information is discounted by the stock market.* Every stock's price is affected not only by news and events, but in anticipation of pending information. When a company is going to announce earnings on Friday, the stock is going to move on Monday through Thursday. If the widespread belief is that the stock will beat analysts' expectations, the price will be driven up. If the opposite expectation dominates, the price will decline. When the outcome is greater than expected in either direction, the price adjusts often violently due to the surprise factor. The market hates surprises, so it invariably overreacts when they pop up.

4. *Market averages must confirm one another before a new trend can be called.* The concept of confirmation is perhaps the most interesting for anyone buying and selling stocks. On the overall market, a change in direction of one average is confirmed when a second average follows suit. The same concept is applied effectively to stocks.

Any number of important indicators can be employed in confirmation. For example, a company's earnings are higher than expected; at the same time, the stock has fallen several points but you read a story revealing that the company is buying back shares of its own stock. (When companies buy their own shares, those shares are permanently retired and can never be resold, which has the effect of helping the value of publicly traded shares, because there are fewer remaining.) You take the decision as a sign that the company itself thinks its stock is a bargain at the current price. The higher earnings are an initial sign, in your opinion, that the share price is going to rise. The buy-back of shares by the company confirms this point of view.

5. *Price trends are confirmed by volume of trading.* Trends mean everything to investors and traders, especially those moving in and out of positions quickly. Swing traders rarely act on singular events. The initial indicator of a change in trend is the three-to-five period direction previously mentioned. But swing traders don't spot a setup until they get confirmation. A two-part confirmation is considered very, very strong. After a three-or-more trend, the trading pattern narrows (meaning the gap between a high and low price in one trading day is very small), and at the same time, the volume of trading spikes to an unusually high level. Although this is a very short-term indicator, it mirrors the market-wide confirmation of the Dow Theory on a smaller scale. When a stock's volume grows, it is due to increased interest among traders, and that usually means a change is coming. A downtrend leads to a volume-based setup of an uptrend, and an uptrend leads to a volume-based setup of a downtrend.

6. *Trends continue until subsequent signals prove that they have ended and new trends have begun.* One dilemma that every investor faces is knowing when to move out of a position. Even if you have perfect timing going in, how do you know when to leave? Here again, as long as all of the indicators remain in place, the trend remains. An uptrend continues up until you receive indicators and a setup that the trend is over. A downtrend continues down until the setup changes.

What if the direction in price changes without any obvious setup? It can happen because random movements are always possible, but it is not the rule. If you see no setup indicating a change in direction but the price turns anyhow, it may be the third of three trends. You will recall that the Dow Theory identifies an uptrend, a downtrend, and a temporary reversal as the third trend. When this occurs, the usual pattern is for price to return to the previously established direction.

It is fair to say that when using the Dow Theory for stock timing, the overall market is broad but individual stock selection is narrow. So the generalized observations of the Dow Theory can also be narrowly applied to time buy and sell decisions for each stock.

Valuable Technical Tests

A fundamental indicator is one based on the numbers, meaning profit or loss and valuation of assets, liabilities, capital stock, and cash flow. A technical indicator is devoted solely to the stock price and the movement of price over time. Many investors use a combination of both fundamental and technical indicators to decide when to buy, hold, or sell stock; and one popular indicator, the P/E ratio, combines the two, involving a technical factor (price) with a fundamental one (earnings).

When you use technical indicators you are relying on ever-moving price trends. The technician believes that price is the most important determining factor in locating bargains and in picking long-term value. Many technicians are also chartists, and believe that you can anticipate future price movement by studying trends on a chart of recent price movement and patterns.

There are hundreds of technical indicators and theories, some very simple and others very complex. The following discussion highlights a few of the basic and most beneficial technical signs, most likely to be useful in combination with fundamental indicators and for the timing of buy and sell decisions. First, though, it is important to note the natural conflict between fundamental and technical approaches to investing.

A fundamental approach relies on historical and recent financial trends in the belief that basic corporate strength and growth mandate which companies are most likely to experience future price growth. As a result, fundamental investors tend to be more conservative and are likely to place money into shares of stock for the long term. A technical approach is based on relatively short-term price movement in the belief that never-ending supply and demand determine how a stock's price changes. While acknowledging that fundamental trends affect price, technicians tend to be more interested in

short-term price movement, and are more likely to act as speculators than as long-term investors.

These observations are never entirely accurate. But it is useful to
be aware of the vast differences between fundamental and technical
analysis when combining both approaches. They are entirely different sets of assumptions, but they are also different aspects of the
same overall tendency. A well-managed company with consistent,
growing fundamentals is also likely to experience low volatility and
ever higher stock prices over time. That is the basic observation
worth remembering.

Among the most useful technical indicators, one of the most
important is the *trading range* of a stock. This is the gap between
the most recent highest and lowest prices at which a stock trades.
There is a tendency for stocks to remain within a well-defined
range, and the breadth of that trading range, or the price gap between high and low price, is also known as *volatility*. The greater
the volatility, the greater the potential for growth and the potential
for loss; in other words, the higher the opportunity/risk. The lower
the volatility, the lower the risk *and* the lower the possibility of price
appreciation.

A trading range may be very consistent or horizontal in nature;
it can also gradually increase or decrease in price levels. The top
level of the trading range is called *resistance* and the bottom is *support*. Three common types of trading ranges are shown in Figure
4-1.

Resistance and support are the cornerstones of most technical
analysis. As long as price remains within the trading range boundaries, it is predictable to some extent. However, when price moves
above resistance or below support, patterns that are called *breakout*,
the whole situation changes. It means a new trading range is being
established or that price is moving temporarily, only to retreat later.

Perhaps as important as breakouts are tests of resistance and
support. As a general technical rule, when price approaches either
edge of the trading range but fails to break through, it anticipates a
price movement in the opposite direction. While breakout is a big
event, failed tests of resistance and support are equally important.
When price fails to move above resistance, it signals that buyers do

FIGURE 4.1. TRADING RANGE

horizontal

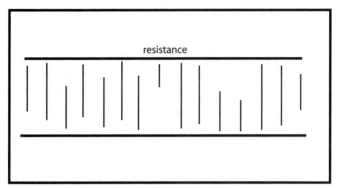

increasing

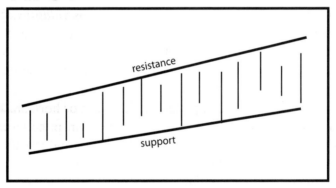

decreasing

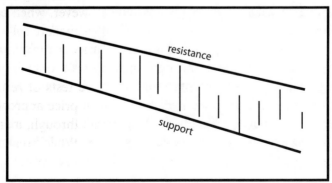

not have enough strength to force prices higher, and when price fails to move below support, it signals that sellers cannot outbid buyers within the established price range.

A common pattern of these resistance and support levels is called *head and shoulders*, so named because it is characterized by three movements, with the middle one higher than the first and third (when testing resistance). A *reverse* head and shoulders occurs on the way down, with the head lower than the first and third shoulders in the pattern. Figure 4-2 shows these patterns.

The pattern in each of these is the same, but the resistance test occurs at the top of the trading range while the support test occurs at the bottom. These patterns are important simply because the attempt to break through resistance or support fails. The "rule" among technicians is that when movement in one direction fails, it usually means movement is going to occur in the opposite direction. When the "shoulders" are closer to the resistance or support levels, the pattern is modified and called a *triple top* or *triple bottom* of the range; the signs are the same, however, with a failure to break through indicating that movement will occur in the opposite direction.

Another important pattern is the gap, which is the distance between one day's closing price and the next day's opening price. Gaps occur in different ways and have different meanings. A summary of the types of gaps is provided in Figure 4-3.

A *common gap* is simply a one-time distance between a subsequent day's trading range and often has no real significance. Technicians, upon seeing a gap, would check a day's trading volume to decide whether it means anything in terms of important price movement.

A *breakaway gap* occurs when the price actually goes through resistance at the top or through support at the bottom, often signaling a change in the trading range itself. However, such gaps often lead to periods of price *congestion* (little if any important movement) and then a retreat to fill the gap.

The *runaway gap* is a series of gaps over a quick period of trading days, all involving price going in the same direction and indicat-

FIGURE 4.2. HEAD AND SHOULDERS PATTERNS

head and shoulders (testing resistance)

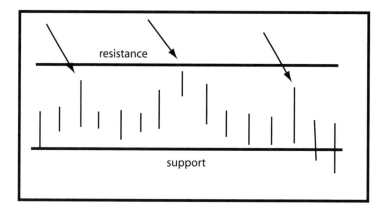

reverse head and shoulders (testing support)

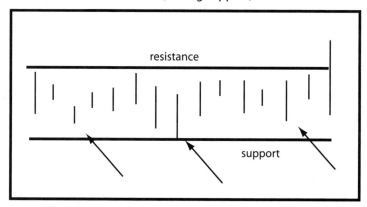

ing a major trend. This often occurs based on rumors like earnings surprises, takeovers, or management changes but the runaway gap is a significant trend and has to be watched carefully.

Finally, an *exhaustion gap* occurs after a strong trend in one direction and precedes movement in the opposite direction. It occurs when sellers exhaust their momentum and buyers enter positions because price has become a bargain. In the opposite direction,

FIGURE 4.3. GAPS

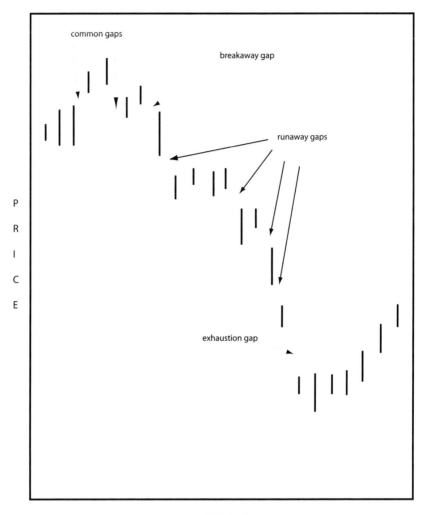

T I M E

an exhaustion gap occurs at the end of a big price run-up, when buyers have exhausted their momentum and traders begin to take profits.

Technical signals can be exciting and revealing. The technicians live from moment to moment, anticipating price movement about to occur. The day-to-day charts are only the starting point; the convenience and technical advantages of the Internet have made it possible for technical analysis on 60-, 15-, and even 5-minute charts. The examination of patterns can occur over a single trading day or literally by the minute. When a technician spots a pattern and makes a move proving to be profitable, it is a satisfying confirmation of the theory itself.

Not as exciting but somewhat more reliable is the range of fundamental indicators. These are based on a company's reported financial outcome, and include tests of profitability as well as capitalization. Fundamental analysis is more conservative and less exciting than technical analysis, but it forms the premise for most people's selection of stocks and decisions about when to buy or sell. The next chapter takes a look at the range of fundamental indicators that every investor needs to understand.

Notes

1 As of December 2005, the DJIA represented 23.8% of the total U.S. market, according to Dow Jones & Company (*www.djindexes.com*).
2 Greiner, Perry, *The History of the Dow Theory*, 1963, Cycles News and Views, at www.cyclesman.com/History of Dow Theory.htm.
3 Alfred Cowles, "Can Stock Market Forecasters Forecast?", *Econometrica*, 1933.

A FEW VALUABLE
FUNDAMENTALS

F inancial statements are complex accounting documents, but you do not need to become an expert at interpreting them; you only need to be able to find a few very important tests to help pick or reject stocks. By studying current ratio in conjunction with debt ratio you can quickly decide how much a corporation depends on stockholders' equity, how much on borrowed money, and more to the point, how well the company manages its working capital.

Beyond financial strength is the question of profitability. Revenue trends can be very revealing. For example, when you see revenues rising but profits falling, that is a red flag. The net return (profits as a percentage of revenues) should be healthy and consistent from one year to the next, and should also be studied on the basis of core earnings.

■ Reading Financial Statements

The financial statements are nothing more than a summary of account balances in a company's books and records. These are shown as of the end of a fiscal quarter or fiscal year.

The *balance sheet* lists the value of all assets (property), liabilities (debt), and net worth (capital stock and retained earnings) as of the last day of the period being reported. The *income statement* shows the sum of all revenues, costs, expenses, and profit or loss for a period of time (a quarter or year). The ending date of this period corresponds with the reporting date of the balance sheet.

The two primary financial statements are often accompanied by a series of supplementary schedules providing additional details: a third statement showing cash flow for the period covered and an extensive number of footnotes, including disclosures and additional information about the highly summarized balance sheet and income statement.

Fundamental analysis should begin with an examination of specific accounts on the balance sheet. This is so-called for two reasons. First, it is a listing of the ending balances of all asset, liability, and net worth accounts. Second, the total of liabilities and net worth accounts exactly equals the total of all asset accounts. This equal balance occurs because under the double-entry system of bookkeeping, every entry contains two sides: a debit and a credit. The books are only in balance when the sum of all debt-balance accounts is the same as the sum of all credit-balance accounts; this provides a simple but effective mathematical control. At the end of the quarter, when the books are "closed" (meaning no additional entries are made until the following period) the sums of all income accounts are zeroed out and moved to the retained earnings account. This means that the balance sheet will also zero out.

The oddities of double-entry bookkeeping aside, it is important to recognize the valuable information you can find on the balance sheet. You do not have to be an expert at financial analysis to extract a few valuable nuggets; in fact, if you invest through an online brokerage service, you probably get free reports as part of the service. For example, Charles Schwab & Company (*www.schwab.com*) gives members free access to Argus Ratings, Goldman Sachs Ratings, Market Edge, Reuters Research, S&P Stock Reports, and Schwab Equity Ratings. Rather than needing to get balance sheets and interpret them, you can easily locate key information. The most complete financial data among this group are found in the S&P

Stock Reports, which provide 10-year summaries of key financial information.

There are numerous sections of the balance sheet, but the three primary sections are (1) assets, (2) liabilities, and (3) net worth. The balancing formula is:

Assets = Liabilities + Net Worth

The features and sections of the balance sheet are summarized in Figure 5-1.

The figure shows a highly summarized version of the balance sheet, but this is often how the report actually is provided in published reports. The details of these accounts and any special disclosures are provided in supplementary schedules and footnotes. The sections of the balance sheet are:

Current assets include any asset convertible to cash within 12 months, including cash, accounts receivable, securities, and inventory.

Long-term assets are also called capital assets and include the purchase value of land and buildings, autos and trucks, and equipment and machinery, as well as a reduction for accumulated depreciation, which is the sum of depreciation expenses claimed each year. All depreciable capital assets are continually depreciated until their book value (original cost less depreciation) equals zero. One exception: Land cannot be depreciated but is always carried at original cost. The way depreciation works brings up one of the oddities of accounting. Asset values decline as they are depreciated, even though some assets (notably real estate) tend to increase in value over time. As a building is depreciated, its value falls until it reaches zero, even though its true market value may be many multiples of its original purchase price.

Other assets may include both tangible and intangible assets. Prepaid and deferred assets are usually expenses that don't apply until a later period, and are set up to be amortized over a number of years. Intangible assets include any covenants or goodwill assets

FIGURE 5.1. BALANCE SHEET

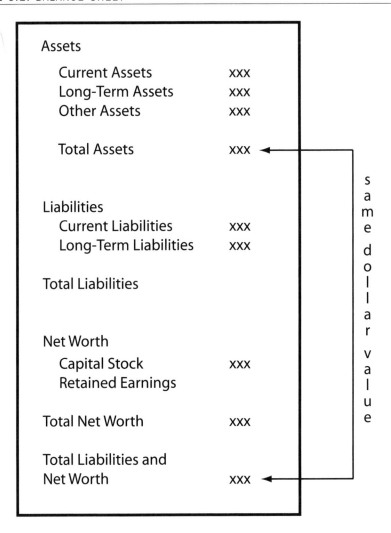

assigned a value but lacking any physical properties. For example, a company will place considerable value on its brand names, reputation, and other nonphysical attributes that are valuable in determining a company's acquisition value.

Current liabilities include all debts that are due to be paid within the next 12 months. This includes 12 months of payments due on long-term loans.

Long-term liabilities are all noncurrent debts, including notes payable and bonds (contractual obligations requiring payment of interest as well as specific repayment of principal).

Capital stock is the fixed value of outstanding shares at the original issue price, even when current market value is different. Capital stock may be common (voting stock is the best-known type) or preferred (more conservative, but nonvoting).

Retained earnings represent the total of all profit or loss reported by the company over its entire existence. At the end of each year, the sum of all revenue, cost, and expense accounts is closed out and the net transferred to the retained earnings account. A profit increases retained earnings, whereas a loss reduces it.

The income statement, also called the operating statement, or more formally, the statement of profit and loss, is described in detail in Chapter 2. The income statement is also a source for valuable fundamental analysis, specifically revenue, costs, expenses, and net profit. Like the balance sheet, it shows a single line for each account, even though a lot of detail is usually involved in arriving at the numbers. The income statement covers a range of time, usually three months (one quarter) or a full fiscal year.

The income statement is usually shown in comparative form. This means that the current quarter is shown first and then the same quarter is shown for the previous year. A full-year report also shows the latest year next to the previous year. This comparative information is valuable as a starting point because it provides an immediate look at how the performance of the current year compares to the most recent previous year. In using online brokerage services, the primary lines of the income statement are shown for many years. The S&P Stock Reports include 10 years of revenue, net profit, and core earnings as well as per-share information, P/E ratio, dividends declared and paid, and many other valuable account totals and ratios.

Most investors will find the free research to be far more practical and useful than a more complex set of financial statements. It is important to understand the concept of how value and history are reported, but for fundamental analysis, using summarized results and ratios online is a much easier, faster, and more accurate approach than paper statements.

The Company's Annual Report: Public Relations Sections

The annual report is actually quite a confusing document. Traditionally, this has been one of the primary sources investors have used for financial and other updates and news. But increasingly, investors have come to recognize that these reports are more public relations than financial in nature, and that it is easier to access financial summaries online, via S&P Stock Reports and other services provided free by online brokerage services.

For anyone who wants to get free annual reports there are many sources. First, you can go to the homepage of any listed company and look for the "investor relations" link. From there you can locate and either download or read the report instantly. One very useful site, *http://www.zpub.com/sf/arl*, links to many good resources for reading annual reports and other useful financial Web sites.

Even though you can get most of your financial information directly from research services, it is useful to see how companies structure their reports, even if your purpose is to read the company's spin on bad news. Many annual reports describe negatives in such a way that they sound very positive. For example, General Motors, one of the old-time U.S. companies in one of the worst capital positions among the DJIA, takes the same positive public relations approach to its annual report that virtually all companies take. Looking at the S&P Stock Reports, you find that GM's net profit and loss has been dismal over three years:

Year	(in millions of dollars) Net Profit (Loss)
2006	$ (1,978)
2005	(10,417)
2004	2,701

Even worse, the company's debt *exceeds* its net worth, meaning the book value of GM is negative. The net worth for the same three years was:

Year	(in millions of dollars) Net Worth
2006	$ (5,441)
2005	14,653
2004	27,726

Even in the face of rising annual net losses and a reduction in the latest reported year of more than *$20 billion* in net worth, the annual report's letter from the president does not explain GM's situation in frank terms. Rather, the tone of the letter is unjustifiably upbeat, including statements like ". . . in 2006, the entire GM team rose up to meet the collective challenge we face . . ." It is not explained what that team effort meant in light of the nearly $2 billion in losses, but the letter also addresses this profitability problem by explaining, "Returning GM to profitability is obviously very important, and we're working intently to achieve that goal."[1]

Remember, the annual report is generated by a company for the primary purpose of attracting and keeping investors. So when there is bad news to report, it is going to be cloaked in the most positive light possible. Anyone reading the statements about GM might think that it was on course for bigger profits than ever, and even if true, it is impossible to tell anything specific from the analysis of the explanation provided by the company and its financial history. The ever-growing levels of debt, which exceeded the company's book value for the first time in 2006, is an extraordinary problem not directly addressed in the explanations.

Several sections of the annual report are devoted mostly to public relations for the company. These include the chairman's letter, sales and marketing, and management discussion and analysis (which includes a confusing mix of required financial disclosures and positive messages). These sections also typically include extravagant photos of happy employees, prosperous fields or plants, and highlighted verbiage emphasizing all of the good news.

Actual financial disclosures are provided in highly technical parts of the document, specifically a multiyear summary of financial highlights (often excluding some of the more important ratios and results that you need and that vary greatly between companies), the auditor's opinion letter, and financial statements. As part of the financial statements, extensive footnotes are included, mostly very technical accounting explanations of how valuation was calculated, items left off the financial statements, and details of some items reported. Most people are not able to follow the footnotes easily, which may run over 100 pages in many cases. Some of the important footnotes include listings of pending litigation, off-balance sheet liabilities, and one-time accounting adjustments or changes made by the company. You will gain far more information from these highly summarized forms by referring to the online analysis.

The problem with financial statements and footnotes is that they are far from user-friendly. The accounting industry is seemingly oblivious to the fact that nonaccountants simply do not understand what these reports reveal or hide, or how to interpret them. There is no incentive for auditing firms to explain their reports in plain English; in fact, given the federal legislation and oversight of the Securities and Exchange Commission (SEC) of the entire accounting industry, auditors have an incentive to disclose only what is absolutely required by law. The legislation passed a few years ago, the Sarbanes–Oxley Act (SOX), imposed new requirements on auditors following a decade of widespread abuse and conflicts of interest in the industry. Unfortunately for investors, today's annual report is not much better than it has been in the past in disclosing information. In fact, the call for transparency has done little to change how annual reports are put together.

One huge problem is the lack of reporting uniformity among companies. Even simple sections of the annual report like "selected" financial highlights varies greatly among companies. Some include three-year summaries only and others list as many as 10 years. The selection of data is also inconsistent, varying widely and making it impossible for anyone to use annual reports to make meaningful comparisons among different companies. The only way to accomplish this is, again, to go directly to online analytical services like the

S&P Stock Reports, where information is reported uniformly. It is unfortunate that listed companies do not work together to create a uniform standard for reporting financial information. It is also a poor record that no effort has been made by the accounting industry, regulatory agencies, or stock exchanges to impose a *requirement* for consistency in format, information, and even titles used in financial reporting.

Investors relying on company-generated annual reports are truly on their own when it comes to gaining information. Even if you send an e-mail to the stockholder relations department of a listed company, you often will not receive a response, depending on your questions and the level of care and concern within the company itself.

▓ Annual Report Disclosure Sections

The disclosures made in annual reports are spread out among several sections. A portion of the management discussion and analysis section is supposed to highlight significant trends and changes. The degree of accuracy varies; few if any companies come out and explain what weaknesses have occurred. In GM's annual report, there is *no mention* of the fact that for the first time, long-term debt went above 100 percent of total capitalization, placing equity in the red. This is extraordinary and significant, but was not included in its management discussion and analysis. The various sections of GM's annual report provide great detail about many financial aspects of operations, including:

Industry, a summary of the U.S. and global automotive market and GM's perception about its role within that market. This is more of a self-promotional section than actual disclosure.

Revenue and net loss is summarized and explained, one of the few purely financial discussions in the report.

Strategy is a detailed discussion of GM's explanation of how its role in the market will emerge; this is also a self-promotional section.

Key factors affecting future and current results is certainly a promising title, and would have been a perfect place to explain GM's long-term debt problems. Unfortunately, this section focuses instead on the "turnaround plan" (marketing and self-promotion), labor negotiations, and the bankruptcy of GM's largest parts supplier, Delphi (DPHIQ).

GMAC—sale of 51 percent interest is a discussion of GM's sale of interests in its financing arm, General Motors Acceptance Corporation.

Investigations explains the ongoing federal audits and investigations of GM's current and past accounting practices.

Liquidity and capital resources is another discussion in which long-term debt could and should have been explained, but there was no mention of the topic. One very important disclosure is that the four major credit rating agencies rate GM's credit as speculative or containing "substantial risk." This is the closest the company comes to talking about its own long-term debt and its dramatic rise in recent years.

Dividends explains the company's policy regarding dividend declarations and payments.

Accounting estimates, standards, and disclosures are mostly technical and include required disclosures.

So even in the "discussion and analysis" of financial results of operations, there is very little in the way of actual discussion and analysis. A lot of important but negative items are excluded, and a lot of marketing and self-promotion are woven throughout the sections.

GM is not the only culprit in the dismal state of affairs of annual statement reporting. Just about every listed company is guilty of the same glossing over of facts and casting bad news in a rosy light. Declining years' sales are often described as "robust, but we can do better" and a net loss is explained away as "a transitional period in our return to profitability." The only conclusion that makes any sense is that you cannot trust management to provide realistic transparency or to discuss its financial condition with integrity. There is no help either from regulators, auditing firms, or stock exchanges. The best source for objective, neutral information is found in independent ratings services.

The "sales and marketing" section of the annual report, in spite of its title, is really just another form of self-promotional material. Even the least competitive company is going to view this section as the place to explain why the company is going to do great things in the future. It also uses this section to explain away declining market share (a growing interest in this industry) and competitive failure (a challenging competitive environment) in the most positive light possible. You really do not gain a sense of the real situation from any material presented in the annual report, where the "rule" is that all of the news is good, and any bad news is going to be qualified or explained away. Thus, terms like restructuring, turnaround, and transition will be abundant in the annual report of companies whose operating results were poor.

The Annual Report's Footnotes

Perhaps the most revealing section of the annual report is the footnotes. Unfortunately, most of the language and discussion is very technical. Footnotes are lengthy and complex, but you can find specific and valuable information if you know what to look for.

The financial statements are highly summarized expressions of valuation (balance sheet) and results from operations (income statement). Depending on a company's industry and any unusual circumstances during the past year, the footnotes can be quite extensive. Footnotes deal with a lot of the details, covering areas such as:

1. *Accounting disclosures and changes.* The most technical types of footnotes deal with the complex discussions of accounting. Many of the financial statement accounts can be interpreted in various ways, so companies need to explain what methods they used. For example, the method used for reporting the value of inventories can drastically affect working capital on the balance sheet as well as

net profit on the income statement. When companies make changes in their valuation or when they have to restate previously reported outcomes, a footnote is where the details are reported.

2. *Details backing up summarized accounts.* Many accounts are reported on the financial statements in single-value summaries, but a lot of detailed information goes into that number. One example is the capital asset section of the balance sheet; another is the general expenses reported on the income statement. Executive compensation is also likely to be reported in a footnote; for example, the highest-paid executives may be listed along with the different kinds of compensation they have been paid. A footnote also is included to explain stock options granted to executives or employees, and extensive information is provided to explain how pension assets and liabilities were calculated. The true liability is usually left out of reported liabilities, so a substantial number can change a company's long-term valuation.

3. *Methods used for valuing of reserves and estimated future income and expenses.* Accounting rules include provisions for specific kinds of reserves. For example, accounts receivable (a current asset constituting money owed to the company by its customers) is reduced by an entry to a reserve for bad debts. This reduces the gross asset value and creates an expense. Many other kinds of reserves are set up to defer income and expenses so as to properly belong in a future year. These kinds of adjustments have been the source for past distortions and misreporting by companies, and among the dozens of abusers most people remember Enron as one of the worst offenders. In varying degrees, companies may practice what is called *sugar bowl accounting,* in which unusually high revenues this year are "deferred" to be recognized later when revenues might not be as positive. The overall effect is to even out the financial summaries.

4. *Assets or liabilities not reported on the balance sheet, or income and expenses not properly reported on the income statement.* One of the greatest problems with modern accounting rules is that companies are allowed to exclude many items from the balance sheet. For example, pension liabilities are not included in the liability

section even when they are substantial. GM would have reported a net negative company value if it booked its pension liabilities. Similarly, many of the core earnings adjustments S&P makes are based on accounting rules allowing companies to overreport income or underreport expenses. For example, capital gains on the sale of company assets should not be included as current-year operating income because it does not recur and is not part of the company's core business. In the past, even large stock option expenses simply disappeared and were never shown as expenses. In years where profits were down, companies have been known to capitalize some expenses to be written off over several years, a decision that exaggerates current profits and misleads investors.

There are many ways that the value and operating results of companies can be distorted. The instances where this is done in violation of the rules are very troubling and SEC investigations have uncovered many. More troubling, however, are the continuing examples of distortions allowed under current accounting rules. For example, companies are not required to report their pension liabilities or the liability for long-term leased equipment. These are very real obligations, but they usually show up only in the footnotes. When the numbers are large, the value of equity is distorted.

5. *Contingent liabilities.* These include pending lawsuits, which may be quite substantial. For example, Altria (Philip Morris) and Merck experienced thousands of pending lawsuits following the tobacco settlements and pharmaceutical judgments of recent years. Most large corporations have some level of contingent liabilities due to lawsuits or losses in loans, subsidiary operations, or acquisition activities.

6. *Mergers and acquisitions activity.* When companies are being acquired or merging with other companies, it may take many months or even years to go through the entire process. Footnotes discuss ongoing merger and acquisition (M&A) activity, current status, and potential impact on the company's value and profit or loss.

Clearly, the footnotes are highly technical and complex, usually running dozens of pages in small print. Many are impossible to decipher for anyone without an accounting background, which is a big part of the problem. Most investors are at a disadvantage in trying to simply understand what is going on, and current reporting rules are a long way from true transparency or from even considering how information for investors can and should be improved. The solution to this problem is to rely on a short list of indicators designed to reveal what is really going on within a company. Distortions can be made to control results in the short term, but over many years, it is impossible to hide the truth. And the long-term trend is key. No ratio or indicator should be looked at by itself, but should be compared to other companies in the same industry, and studied for at least five years, preferably 10 years. Only by tracking the trend can you see what has occurred in the past and in the most recent report. This is the best way to overcome the complexity of the accounting methods in use today.

Combining Technical and Fundamental Analysis

It makes sense to adopt a view of *caveat emptor* in the modern stock market. Relying on the published financial statements of companies is simply not a wise idea. There are too many ways that the numbers can be manipulated within what is approved and allowed. Regulatory agencies, stock exchanges, and auditing firms are all in agreement about the flaws in the liberal interpretation of accounting rules. There are many sound reasons for the complexities of this system; unfortunately, it means that you have to do your own homework. Fortunately, a lot of good basic information is available and is free through the research and analysis provided as part of online brokerage accounts.

Combining both technical and fundamental analysis enables you to view both financial and price-based information, and to use each to confirm the other. You will discover that strong and consistent financial statements translate to low-volatility stock history. The two are directly related. You will also see several shared attributes among well-managed companies whose stock is available at a value price. These attributes include consistent rise in dividend payments over many years, a moderately low degree of price volatility, consistency in the financial reports themselves, and little or no adjustments between reported earnings and core earnings. Collectively, these are the primary signs of well-managed companies.

Financial outcome is best viewed over many years. When you see steadily increasing revenues and net profits, you get a sense of reliability in the numbers. Every company goes through brief periods where the stock is out of favor, thus a stock price might falter even when the fundamentals remain strong. However, as long as all of the fundamental signs are unchanged, the momentary effect of market value will be a passing event. Long term, the fundamentals are the key to sound stock selection.

Market-wide trends will affect stock trading ranges even when long-term fundamental results are strong and consistent. Two good examples of this are Wal-Mart and Microsoft. Both are well-managed, successful companies that dominate their industries. Wal-Mart's stock price weakened toward the end of its 10-year history ending with fiscal 2007, reflecting retail industry weakness overall; in fact, Wal-Mart underperformed its industry in 2007 due to predictions that "hyper-store" sales were going to weaken over time. In spite of these kinds of predictions, Wal-Mart continued to expand internationally, adding hundreds of new outlets in many countries.

Microsoft also experienced strong revenue and profit growth while its stock price reflected market perceptions differently. Trading as high as $60 per share in 1999, stock prices settled down to as low as $21 per share in fiscal 2006. There has been no obvious weakness in Microsoft's fundamentals; in fact, growth in revenues and profits has been consistent and strong. The fact that stock price range did not change very much between 2001 and 2007 reflects the market conditions and the industry more than Microsoft itself. Given the history of both of these companies, checking both technical and fundamental indicators is the wisest methodology for investors.

A summary of the 10-year history of revenues, net profit, and price ranges for Wal-Mart and Microsoft is provided in Table 5-1.

There seems to be an odd nonreaction in the case of Microsoft between the stock price and the revenue/profits, notably between

TABLE 5-1. FUNDAMENTAL AND TECHNICAL HISTORY

Company	Year	In Millions of Dollars		Stock Prices	
		Revenue	Net Profit	High	Low
Wal-Mart	2007	$348,650	$12,178	$52	$42
	2006	312,427	11,231	55	42
	2005	285,222	10,267	61	51
	2004	256,329	8,861	60	46
	2003	244,524	8,039	64	44
	2002	217,799	6,671	59	42
	2001	191,329	6,295	69	41
	2000	165,013	5,575	70	39
	1999	137,634	4,430	41	19
	1998	117,958	3,526	21	11
Microsoft	2007	$51,122	$14,065	$36	$27
	2006	44,282	12,599	30	21
	2005	39,788	12,254	28	24
	2004	36,835	8,168	30	25
	2003	32,187	9,993	30	23
	2002	28,365	7,829	35	21
	2001	25,296	7,721	38	21
	2000	22,956	9,421	59	20
	1999	19,747	7,785	60	34
	1998	14,484	4,490	36	16

Source: Standard & Poor's Stock Reports

1999 and 2001 and again between 2003 and 2007. Note how in the most recent series of years, revenue and profits rise strongly each year, but the stock price remains unchanged until 2007. It is as though a delayed reaction dominates on the technical side. However, the point to remember about this kind of comparison is that over many years, consistent growth and fundamental strength translates to growth in stock prices. The Wal-Mart historical comparison is more in line with this observation than that of Microsoft. In fact, the high price for fiscal year 2007 was just about the same as it had been 10 years earlier, at $36 per share. The low end of the range, in comparison, was far stronger. In both cases, it may be true that some kind of saturation point was reached after 10 years of growth, but until an actual slowdown occurs in the revenue/profits trend, there is every reason to believe that the stock's price ranges will continue to expand.

Combining both technical and fundamental analysis makes sense because it broadens your point of view. By studying past history you can see how the future is likely to go. For this reason, it is wise to come up with a short list of indicators to review in combination with one another. They collectively serve as a broad view of fundamental and technical change, as well as providing many forms of confirmation.

Basic List of 10 Indicators Every Investor Needs

Everyone has their own preferences about which indicators to use. Some are undeniably valuable for distinguishing between stocks in one manner or another. The list that follows includes one combined, two technical, and seven fundamental ratios. Most people will not want to deal with more than 10 indicators; some will be confident with fewer. All of these, used in combination, can be useful in developing your investment portfolio.

COMBINED TECHNICAL/FUNDAMENTAL INDICATOR

The *P/E ratio* is popular and revealing because of easy comprehension: It quickly casts the condition of stock in terms of valuation and is a great indicator for comparisons between stocks and to a standard.

The standard recommended for most people is to limit yourself to stocks with price per earnings (P/E) under 25. Consider what this means: When P/E is 25, the current price is 25 times earnings. So if the stock's price is $50 per share and earnings per share (EPS) is $2, the P/E is 25:

$$\$50 \div \$2 = 25$$

Consider what would happen if the stock were to rise to $100 per share. At that point, P/E would be 50. Clearly, the stock is more of a bargain at $50 per share, especially if EPS remains unchanged. The perception of future value is reflected in P/E. Some highly popular stocks have grown so quickly that their P/E moved high as well. For example, Google's (GOOG) P/E ranged between 52 and 33 in 2006, and in its previous fiscal year (2005), went as high as 89. So at some point in 2005, investors were willing to pay 89 times EPS for shares of Google. The price since then has proven to have been a wise move, with the stock more than doubling to over $700 per share in 2007, but the point to remember is that the higher the P/E, the higher the market risk.

TECHNICAL INDICATORS

On the technical side, two indicators are worth checking. First is the *trading range* itself. If you have tracked a stock over 10 years or more, you will see the change in the trading range. It is fair to say that a climbing range is positive and a declining range is highly negative. Many investors buy stock based solely on today's price, without even considering whether the market price has grown or declined over 10 years. This common mistake—thinking about the purchase price as a starting point—leads to many cases of poor timing or simply poor selection. For example, compare two well-known companies, Eastman Kodak and Johnson & Johnson (JNJ). Table 5-2 shows the 10-year history of the trading range for each of these companies.

Both of these histories are dramatic, but in opposite directions. These price ranges are summarized graphically in Figure 5-2.

The 10-year changes in trading range demonstrate significant differences between these two companies. Whereas Kodak's market value has declined steadily, JNJ has experienced a steady rise, more than doubling in market value ranges.

A second technical indicator to track is *trading volatility*. This is simply the breadth between resistance (high price) and support (low price) within the trading range. However, there is more. The volatil-

TABLE 5-2. TRADING RANGE COMPARISON: 10 YEARS

Company	Year	Stock Price High	Low
Eastman Kodak	2007	$ 31	$19
	2006	35	21
	2005	35	24
	2004	41	20
	2003	28	26
	2002	50	24
	2001	68	35
	2000	80	57
	1999	89	58
	1998	95	53
Johnson & Johnson	2007	$69	$57
	2006	70	60
	2005	64	49
	2004	59	48
	2003	66	41
	2002	61	40
	2001	53	33
	2000	53	39
	1999	45	32
	1998	34	24

Source: Standard & Poor's Stock Reports (prices rounded)

ity factor also distinguishes between low-risk stocks and high-risk stocks. By definition, low risk means that the trading range remains about the same size. For example, a stock trading within a 10-point range last year still trades in a 10-point range this year and has not deviated from that breadth. Ideally, the trading range has been inching toward higher price ranges during that period. In a high-risk stock, the range changes often. It may also be characterized by a number of breakouts above resistance and below support, with prices retreating soon thereafter, and by frequent trading gaps. These gaps themselves are not negative indicators but when they occur often, and when price moves quickly beyond its trading range

FIGURE 5.2. 10-YEAR TRADING RANGE COMPARISON

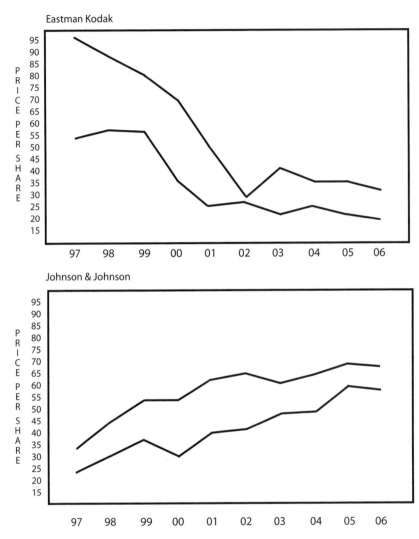

Source: S&P Stock Reports

in a gap pattern and then returns, it is an indication of high volatility. A related factor is trading volume. When you see volume changing from one day to the next, and even spiking to unusually high levels with dramatic price movement, it implies high-risk conditions.

FUNDAMENTAL INDICATORS

The fundamentals are the mainstay for many moderate and conservative investors. But because there are so many indicators available, no one can follow them all. In fact, with too much information, you lose the ability to identify a clear and obvious signal. Thus, you need to reduce the number of indicators whenever possible. Another principle worth observing is that singular indicators are not as valuable as a dual analysis of two related indicators.

The first fundamental indicator is a combined test of both working capital and capitalization. By watching *current ratio* and the *debt ratio*, you will be able to keep an eye on some very basic money movement within the company. Watching these two indicators together is absolutely necessary.

Current ratio is a comparison between current assets (convertible to cash within the next 12 months) and current liabilities (payable within the next 12 months). To compute, divide the current assets value by current liabilities, as shown in Figure 5-3.

For example, a company's current assets are $62,558 and current liabilities are $37,004. The current ratio is:

$$\$62,558 \div \$37,004 = 1.7$$

The current ratio "standard" is that 2 or higher is considered excellent and depending on how much inventory is involved, a ratio between 1 and 2 is also acceptable. However, these are generalizations and by itself, current ratio reveals only one aspect of how well the company manages its working capital. The ratio demonstrates over time how much liquidity is available to pay current debts.

FIGURE 5.3. CURRENT RATIO

The current ratio should be tracked along with the most important capitalization ratio, known as the *debt/equity ratio*. This is a
comparison between long-term debt and equity. Every company
and industry has different standards for this ratio. However, over
time you may see a creeping effect, in which debt grows. GM experienced a growing debt ratio over a decade, resulting in debt over
100 percent of equity. This is an extreme case. Microsoft, at the
other end of the spectrum, carries no long-term debt on its balance
sheet. Also called the debt-to-capital ratio, this is computed by adding together the long-term debt and the shareholder's equity to find
total capitalization. The long-term debt was previously explained. A
quick review: A company currently has $92,064 in long-term debt
and $117,680 in equity. Total capitalization is $209,744 ($92,064
+ $117,680). The debt ratio is:

$92,064 ÷ $209,744 = 43.9%

If this ratio were fairly consistent over many years, then the
trend is acceptable. A falling debt ratio is always preferable because
less debt translates to lower interest expense and more capital available for expansion and dividend payments.

Watching current ratio and debt ratio together is crucial, because a hidden trend can emerge if you are not cautious. A company
wishing to maintain its current ratio during years when it is losing
money may easily increase its long-term debt and hold onto the
borrowed funds in cash. Even as the financial condition deterio-
rates, the current ratio can be held at the same level but long-term
debt continues to rise. In other words, by allowing long-term debt
to rise each year, a company can report declining profits and even
losses, but its current ratio remains consistent. So if you check only
the current ratio, you will miss this trend.

An example of this occurred over the 10-year history of Eastman Kodak, from 1997 through fiscal 2006. This is summarized in
Table 5-3.

There is a dramatic trend underway in this 10-year history.
However, if you give great weight to working capital as a primary
indicator and you track only the current ratio, Kodak was able to

TABLE 5-3. CURRENT RATIO AND DEBT RATIO ANALYSIS

Eastman Kodak:

Year	Net Income (in millions of dollars)	Current Ratio	Debt Ratio
2007	$ −600	1.1	66.2%
2006	− 1,455	1.1	58.4
2005	81	1.1	32.7
2004	238	1.0	41.4
2003	793	0.8	29.5
2002	$ 76	0.9	36.5%
2001	1,407	0.9	25.0
2000	1,392	0.9	0
1999	1,390	0.9	11.1
1998	5	1.1	15.6

Source: Standard & Poor's Stock Reports

maintain approximately a 1.0 ratio through the entire decade. All is well, or so it would appear. When you study the deterioration in net income, you see a downward spiral underway. With less profit, and in the two most recent years, net losses, how can Kodak maintain its 1.1 current ratio? The answer is found in ever-higher levels of long-term debt. Ten years before, debt represented only 15.6 percent of total capitalization; at the end of fiscal 2006, this had grown by over 400 percent to 66.2 percent of total capitalization. This is not a positive trend by any means, and for stockholders it is very troubling—in spite of the positive current ratio history.

The second and third fundamental indicators deal with dividends. These are the *current yield* and the 10-year history of *dividend growth*. Current yield, you will recall, is calculated by dividing the annual dollar value of dividends by current share price. For example, total dividends are declared at $1 per share, payable each quarter (for a total of $4 per year), and current share price is $80 per share. So current dividend yield is:

$$\$4 \div \$80 = 5.0\%$$

As a minimum standard, current yield should be set at a reasonable level. Dividend yield will end up representing a significant portion of your overall investment return, so dividends should not be ignored. Additionally, a company's ability to pay an attractive dividend is a very positive attribute. A company cannot continue paying dividends unless it has profits and positive cash flow. For example, you may decide to isolate your search only to companies with 4 percent or better annual dividends. This will reduce your selection considerably.

The history of *dividend growth* is best studied over 10 years. Those companies that have increased dividends every year for 10 years or more ("dividend achievers") are among the best-managed and most successful companies available to the public. This provides you with a secondary dividend-related qualifier in narrowing down your list of stock candidates for inclusion in your portfolio.

The fourth basic fundamental indicator is a comparison between revenue and net profits. There are several points worth checking in the multiple-year trend, including growth of revenues compared to changes in profits, the rate of growth, and the question of why it sometimes occurs that revenues increase but profits fall, a very troubling and negative change in the trend. Focusing only on ever-higher revenues is worthless unless the company is also able to take ever-higher portions of revenues to the bottom line.

For example, look at the 10-year history summarizing revenue and net income for two companies, American Airlines (AMR) and Amazon.com (AMZN). These are shown in Table 5-4.

Both companies show a very disturbing trend, and this highlights the importance of tracking revenue and net income together. American Airlines has had a high volume of revenue that increased throughout the decade. However, its profits have never been impressive and, in fact, most recent years reported net losses. Amazon's history has always been characterized by very low profit margins, in fact, it has only shown a profit during the four most recent years. The troubling aspect here is that in 2006, although total revenue jumped considerably and annual revenue growth was spectacular, net income for the three latest years declined. Even though the company became profitable, increased revenue has been accompanied by ever-smaller net. Seek companies whose revenues

TABLE 5-4. REVENUE AND INCOME TRENDS

| Company | Year | In Millions of Dollars | |
		Revenue	Net Profit
American Airlines	2006	$22,563	$ 231
	2005	20,712	− 861
	2004	18,645	− 761
	2003	17,440	−1,228
	2002	17,299	−2,523
	2001	18,963	−1,762
	2000	19,703	779
	1999	17,730	656
	1998	19,205	1,306
	1997	18,570	985
Amazon.com	2006	$10,711	$ 190
	2005	8,490	333
	2004	6,921	588
	2003	5,264	35
	2002	3,933	− 150
	2001	3,122	− 577
	2000	2,762	−1,411
	1999	1,640	− 720
	1998	610	− 125
	1997	148	− 28

Source: Standard & Poor's Stock Reports

and net income grow each year. When you see higher top-line results with lower bottom-line results, it is a negative trend.

The next indicator worth following is *fundamental volatility*, the
degree to which the numbers vary from one year to the next. For
example, compare the low volatility of Wal-Mart with the much
higher fundamental volatility of DuPont in the same decade. These
results are summarized in Table 5-5.

Notice how Wal-Mart's revenues climb steadily year after year
and, more to the point, so do net profits. However, DuPont's revenues have been relatively flat for most of the period, while net income was inconsistent. Compare the 1997 result, in which net was
5.3 percent of revenue to the next year (6.7 percent) and the year

TABLE 5-5. FUNDAMENTAL VOLATILITY COMPARISONS

Company	Year	In Millions of Dollars	
		Revenue	Net Profit
Wal-Mart	2007	$348,650	$12,178
	2006	312,427	11,231
	2005	285,222	10,267
	2004	256,329	8,861
	2003	244,524	8,039
	2002	217,799	6,671
	2001	191,329	6,295
	2000	165,013	5,575
	1999	137,634	4,430
	1998	117,958	3,526
E.I. DuPont de Nemours	2006	$ 27,421	$ 3,148
	2005	26,639	2,053
	2004	27,340	1,780
	2003	26,996	1,002
	2002	24,006	1,841
	2001	24,726	4,328
	2000	28,268	2,314
	1999	26,918	219
	1998	24,767	1,648
	1997	45,079	2,405

Source: Standard & Poor's Stock Reports

after that, 1999, when net was 0.8 percent. The most recent year, 2006, reported 11.5 percent net income. With flat revenues, the company's net income is highly inconsistent.

Another important fundamental test is a comparison between *net income* and *core net income*. Examples of these variations have been previously provided, and the important point to emphasize is the underlying significance. When you see very low core earnings adjustments in companies (such as Wal-Mart's, which is miniscule), this is a very positive sign. When you see volatile core earnings adjustments (such as the multibillion adjustments for General Motors) it indicates accounting problems or inconsistency in the financial reports.

Two final fundamental indicators to keep in mind are the company's *competitive and management status* and its *credit rating*. One of the basic standards of value investing is to concentrate on companies with exceptional management that are strong leaders in their industry sectors. Well-managed, strongly competitive companies are more likely to perform better than average even in soft or downturning markets. Credit rating is often overlooked, and that is a mistake. Few investors pause to realize that GM has a very poor credit rating so that its corporate bonds in 2007 had junk bond status. Similarly, American Airlines, with a 2006 debt ratio of 105.3 percent of total capitalization, had its debt rated Caa2 (in poor standing) in 2007. In those instances where credit ratings are in the junk bond classification, investors have to wonder whether it makes sense to invest money. This is especially true when long-term debt has grown so high that it puts equity in the negative.

SEVEN FUNDAMENTAL INDICATORS

1. Current ratio combined with debt ratio
2. Current yield
3. Dividend growth
4. Revenue and net profits
5. Fundamental volatility
6. Competitive and management status
7. Credit rating

The indicators worth following are valuable only when tracked on a comparative basis between companies, and over many years (at least five, preferably 10 years). As a matter of basic risk, knowing a company's financial strength or weakness and being able to identify bargains versus overpriced stocks is a good starting point for building a strong portfolio. In the next chapter, the big issue of risk is explored, both in historical context and to explain the various kinds of risk everyone faces in the stock market.

▓ Note

1 Annual report, 2006, *www.gm.com*.

IDENTIFYING THE RISK

T he famous market illogic known as "tulip mania" occurred hundreds of years ago in Holland. Speculation in tulip bulbs was so widespread that entire fortunes were invested in single bulbs. It was not until the whole thing came crashing down that people realized how risky the entire matter was. This history has relevance today.

Most investors know only about the most obvious form of risk, called "market risk." This is the risk in losing value due to a decline in a stock's market price. However, many other forms of risk need to be examined in order to compare opportunities in the market. Risk also extends to economic factors; for example, utility companies' stock value is affected directly by interest rates because utilities rely heavily on debt capitalization. A specific sector also may be characterized by certain identical risks, such as sensitivity to interest rates or common trends. Thus, the investor needs to study risk from the larger view to ensure that risk is either minimal or that different risks are spread among dissimilar issues.

Risk management in this sense may also be termed "opportunity management," because risk and opportunity are different aspects of the same condition. A change in risk posture often first shows up in earnings, followed by changes in dividend yield. Thus, risk adjustments also serve as a form of primary movement or change in a stock's trend; for example, the practical application of the Dow Theory.

Lessons to Be Learned from Holland

In the 1630s, nearly 400 years ago, an odd occurrence in Holland provided a valuable historical lesson. Speculators invested literally fortunes in single tulip bulbs as a market went crazy—prices ran up and common people became rich—and then the whole thing crashed and all of those fortunes were lost.

This strange event, known as tulip mania, was short in duration, but holds valuable lessons for every investor today. It demonstrates how crowds think and how both greed and fear dominate any market where money is involved.

By their nature, tulip bulbs are scarce. From a seed, it may take 5–10 years to produce a flower, and another 3–5 years for it to evolve into a flowering bulb. Rarity is further defined by the color markings in variegated tulips. Ironically, these colors are the result of viruses that reduce the number of offsets, making them even more rare. In 1635, an important change occurred in the tulip market. Rather than selling flowering bulbs once produced, the market began trading in tulips while they were still in the ground, and a lot of this trading took place by promissory note rather than an actual exchange of cash. The market evolved into a type of tulip futures situation. Speculation regarding time to maturity, weight, and quality often created several hundred percent growth in value, so that speculators saw great potential in this futures market. By 1636, the market itself had grown considerably following a year of depressed prices, and many more people could afford to get into the tulip speculation business.

As many speculative markets do, this one accelerated to the point that prices rose to irrational levels. To provide some perspective on the wild speculation, a 1635 sale of 40 bulbs went as high as 100,000 florin. In comparison, one ton of butter was worth 100 florin. Some bulbs, like the best-known and most sought-after

Semper Augustus, were sold for as much as 6,000 florin (over $4,000) for a single bulb.

The market became so exaggerated that traders began selling tulips that had only recently been planted and even made sales for tulips not yet planted, a dubious move called *windhandel* (wind trade). But by the beginning of 1637, the speculative bubble had reached its peak and prices would not rise any further. As it always happens, the entire bubble burst quite rapidly and suddenly, many holders of futures contracts discovered overnight that their speculative holdings were worthless. Thousands of investors, traders, and speculators lost everything.

The obvious lessons gained in hindsight are clear. Speculators of the period mortgaged their homes to get into the game and committed themselves to unimaginable debt, all in the belief that they were going to get rich. Three of the important lessons are:

1. *Irrational speculation never anticipates the end.* This occurs time and time again. Few speculators, in the middle of a speculative frenzy, stop to think about the actual risk they live with, and virtually no one who is making big profits wonders about when it will all end. Most speculators merely assume that they will magically know exactly when the market is about to crash, and plan to get out right before that happens. But it never works that way.

2. *Few speculators set prices for themselves to take profits and get out.* The "greed factor" in speculative frenzies dominates people and the way they think. Surely everyone has heard the clear-headed and rational advice to set goals, and when those goals are reached, sell and get out. It would be smart to do so, but it doesn't work in times of manic speculation. The only fear speculators have at the time is that they might get out too early and miss out on even more profits. So instead of saying "I will double my investment and then sell," it is more common for speculators to churn their profits into ever-higher levels of risk. Thus, even with amazing profits in hand, the tendency is to leave it at risk until the inevitable 100 percent loss occurs.

3. *Logic goes out the window when profits appear easy to make.* The very fact that speculative bubbles exist turns otherwise logical

and even cautious investors into irrational, greedy, and "blind" speculators. During tulip mania, many people who had never invested before put all caution aside and made vast fortunes on paper, took those profits, and reinvested them into more future holdings, apparently oblivious to the potential risks. There is something about human nature that allows people to put logic aside when potential riches appear, and to suspend risk tolerance standards to chase easy money.

The historical events of tulip mania demonstrate how people act in any market where money exists. The primary human emotions at such times are greed and fear. Greed allows people to see no end in sight to their profit potential, right up to the point where it all evaporates. Fear replaces greed overnight, and is equally irrational.

The value in remembering tulip mania is that in the stock market, this kind of illogical activity—ruled by greed on the way in and by fear and panic on the way out—is possible today. Yes, even with the vast free information on the Internet and sophisticated trading systems everyone hears about, greed and fear remain the primary emotions in any market, most notably the stock market. Even so, perceptions about market troubles can also be irrational. For example, the cyclical real estate market in 2005 and 2006 was said to be in a speculative bubble that was about to burst. In fact, actual bubbles existed but only in isolated areas. Most real estate markets, all of which operate in a uniquely local manner, were not affected by the speculative bubble. Credit problems that came to light in 2007 were of far greater concern to anyone needing a mortgage. But like all markets, the cycle declined and then rose. The greed of tulip mania and the panic of the 2005–2007 real estate markets were both very irrational.

The history of the stock market provides many examples where greed and fear also caused grief, and it all relates to perception versus reality of *risk* and how it works. At the turn of the twenty-first century, the U.S. stock markets went through a speculative craze reflecting the modern era, specifically relating to the all-new Internet and its potential for vast future profits. This infamous "dot .com bubble" will be remembered for many years to come.

■ Modern Market Crazes: Greed and Fear

The lessons of tulip mania are interesting, and without a doubt, those unfortunate speculators who lost entire fortunes were able to look back and puzzle at how they lost perspective. But there are many similarities between seventeenth-century Holland and twenty-first-century America. Tulip mania was not an aberration, only an extreme example of the same tendencies that continue to this day.

Between 1995 and 2000, a similar euphoria took over a large segment of the U.S. market. This has been termed the "dot.com bubble." Relatively new stocks in the "Internet sector" grew rapidly in value with individual investors buying up shares and large sums of venture capital adding fuel to the fire.

One of the most puzzling aspects of the dot.com bubble was that many of the companies whose value soared in the period seemed to exist only on paper and did not provide a specific product or service. Much as the mysterious but beautiful tulip bulb attracted speculators 400 years before, the exciting and promising profits of dot.com had a similar effect. Even those dot.com companies that did have products often set up unrealistic business models. And many were formed by relatively young and inexperienced first-time business owners.

At the time, the ability to set up an attractive Web page was more valuable than understanding how to build and grow a business. In fact, rather than the traditional concept of offering excellent products at competitive prices, a new and different model dominated the dot.com industry: Sell at a loss to gain dominance in the industry, and support ever-higher losses with both equity and debt capitalization. The purpose was to crush competition and grow rapidly, with the idea that profits could be created later, when the dot.com "owned" its market niche. On paper, it's not a bad idea, assuming that there is some point where the losses can, indeed, be turned around into profits. Unfortunately, so many entrepreneurs accepted this model that any type of valuation became impossible in the market.

In hindsight, the dot.com craze was short-lived but shared many characteristics with the tulip craze of the 1600s, as well as speculation in railroads in the 1840s, and later, in the auto industry, transistor electronics, time-sharing computers, and biotechnology. But like all crazes, no matter the duration, dot.com came to an end rather suddenly. This is typical of how crazes go! First, they dominate and appear permanent. Then, quite suddenly, they disappear.

At least when a bubble is based on a product like transistor radios or automobiles, there is a quantifiable factor identifying market saturation points. All markets are finite, so companies can sell only so many transistor radios. Even tulips exist only in a limited quantity, so there is some tangible justification for value to change. But the dot.com bubble was different. There was so much competition, and so many identical business models fighting for the same competitive market, that it became impossible for most of them to survive. Like all bubbles, a few early successes generated ever-greater interest. When people saw early speculators becoming millionaires overnight, more and more people wanted to get in as well. It is ironic that the actual business model became secondary. Some companies might as well have been selling tulip bulbs online.

Only in a bubble environment is it possible for a company to make an initial public offering even though it has never reported a profit, and has not been in business for very long—and be able to not only raise money but also see its stock value soar. The growing value of dot.com stocks was most visible on the NASDAQ Composite Index, which peaked on March 10, 2000, at a level twice its size only one year earlier. Such spectacular rises in markets is a warning sign, but typically, people invested in the dot.com industry refused to consider the possibility that the good times would ever end.

No single reason can be cited for the rapid demise of the dot.com business. Irrational panic over the widely hyped Y2K problems (which did not materialize), sell-off of stocks in many established companies like IBM and other technology-based growing concerns, and anticipation about the outcome of a big lawsuit against the leading software company (*United States v. Microsoft*) all added to the crash of the dot.com business. But the primary reason was the lack of tangible value and the unrealistic price run-ups in preceding months. In three trading days ending March 15, 2000, the NASDAQ lost about 9 percent of its composite index value.

Following closely on the dot.com craze was a period in which many big companies were reported to have accounting irregularities. Best known in this group was Enron, but many communications and IT companies had problems as well. WorldCom had exaggerated its profits in the billions of dollars and filed the largest bankruptcy in U.S. history. Other companies with problems included Global Crossing (GLBC), JDS Uniphase (JDSU), and NorthPoint Communications (NPNTQ). While this was going on, dot.com problems led to the dissolution of many companies, and charges of widespread fraud surfaced. Big Wall Street firms that had underwritten many of the initial offerings were fined millions of dollars; these included Citigroup (C) and Merrill Lynch (MER), among others.

Several years after the dot.com craze had quieted down, many market observers continued to be concerned. Rapid growth of companies like Google (with a P/E above 55 by October 2007) doubled its stock price in less than two years. Other high-P/E companies in 2007 included Apple (AAPL) (48), Sun Microsystems (JAVA) (42), and Yahoo! (56). However, all of these are extremely overvalued, especially compared to competitors like Microsoft, with a P/E of only 24.

Several years following the dot.com era, many of the survivors have been buying up competition. For example, Google bought YouTube and eBay (EBAY) bought Skype and PayPal. Other companies notable in the dot.com era included search engines (Altavista, Excite, Lycos); online brokerages (Ameritrade, E*TRADE); consumer products (Amazon.com, eToys, Pets.com, Priceline.com, Travelocity); and consumer services (GeoCities, InfoSpace, mortgage.com, Netscape, Telefonica).

Market Risk

The specific timing, length, and other features of bubbles in the markets vary, but one thing remains the same: market risk. This refers to the risk that your investment will fall as stock price declines. In extreme cases (like Enron or WorldCom), you could lose all or most of your investment capital. Market risk is impossible to avoid, but by remembering some of the fundamental guidelines and applying analysis wisely, you can avoid unpleasant surprises.

Rather than reacting with the two most common emotions in the market (greed and fear), experienced investors follow a few sensible rules:

1. *Never follow the crowd, especially when emotions run high.* As difficult as this advice is to heed, it is essential to success in the market. The overall tendency is to experience fear when prices fall, and to act impulsively by selling to cut losses and to buy, buy, buy when prices are rising. These emotions—greed and fear— absolutely dominate the market, causing a lot of grief. Keeping a cool head, taking a step back, and waiting before entering a trade impulsively is a wise move. If you have picked stocks wisely, employing tried-and-true indicators, there is no need to sell in a panic; in fact, a decline in price that seems extreme could present a buying opportunity. Also resist the temptation to jump into speculative buying when prices rise quickly. The more they rise, the closer you are to the top, and the more likely a correction will occur.

2. *Be willing to lose a few golden opportunities in exchange for long-term certainty.* Without a doubt, you are going to experience losses; remember, it is easy to convince yourself that your entry price is a starting point, when in reality it is only the current price in an ever-changing series of price movements. Some losses are inevitable. By the same logic, you do not have to seize each and every opportunity that comes along. If you try, it is virtually guaranteed that you will suffer more losses rather than fewer losses. It is wiser to take some time and make decisions without the pressure of the moment. Apply your analysis to the long term, don't buy unless the basics make sense, and delay decisions until you are sure the decision of whether to buy or sell makes sense given the current price and trend, *and* is based on thorough analysis.

3. *Set specific profit* and *loss limit goals and follow your own rules.* The biggest mistake investors make regarding market risk is

failing to set specific exit strategies for themselves, or to take steps to protect their positions. As a consequence, they do not have any idea about when to close positions. If a stock's price is changing rapidly, stop loss orders (automatic orders based on the stock reaching a predetermined price) make sense. It creates an exit point without requiring a separate decision. If you do not set an exit price for yourself, you won't know when to take profits or cut losses. If prices rise, the tendency is to hold off, hoping the prices will rise even more. If prices fall, the tendency is to hold off hoping to get back to the starting point. In this almost universal scenario, when and where do you exit?

Market risk appears simple and easy to understand. But human nature is not. Market risk, which is dominated by human emotions, tends to become very complex. Investors have paper profits and delay making a decision, only to end up realizing losses because they end up making decisions at the worst possible times. The market is not going to conform to wishful thinking, and the reason most investors lose money is simply because they react to signals in the way opposite of their best interests. It is irrational to buy at the top as well as to sell at the bottom, but that is how the course of events goes too often.

Market risk is not difficult to understand, but acting at the right time and making decisions contrary to the "group think" of the market is the only way to reduce that risk. In respect of the emotional tendency of the market as a whole, market risk is the most complex form of risk you face. But it is not the only risk; there is more.

■ Inflation and Tax Risk

People tend to underestimate the double effect of inflation and taxes. Even when the current inflation rate is relatively low, it is easy to overlook. In fact, if you don't think about inflation and taxes together in the way that this "double whammy" impacts on your profitability, then you probably will not make a profit in the market.

An example: Let's say you choose a stock yielding no dividend and invest $5,000 at $50 per share. You are confident that your money will grow. Over the course of a year, the price of the stock rises to $53 per share. But did you really make a profit? If we add a couple of modest assumptions about inflation and taxes, you might discover that you are *losing* money. If the rate of inflation is 3 percent, you lose $150 in spending power of your $5,000 investment. Now if you apply the combined federal and state effective tax rate, you will need to reduce your profits accordingly. For example, if you pay 33 percent federal and another 6 percent state income tax, your combined tax liability is 39 percent. If you were to sell and take your $300 profit, you would be penalized $117. The loss from inflation ($150) and taxes ($117) equals $267. So your true post-inflation and post-tax gain over one year would be only $33, or 0.7 percent. (This example does not assume a reduced rate for capital gains and also makes no adjustment in the event you do not sell the stock.)

In Chapter 1, you saw how a break-even rate of return applied to investments, and Table 1-3 showed how some gross returns were reduced by inflation and taxes. Table 1-3 is duplicated here in Table 6-1.

The risk of inflation and taxes is considerable. Investors may easily delude themselves by thinking they are doing well by earning 3 or 4 percent per year on their investments, but it is not always true. Even a 26 percent effective tax rate and 3 percent inflation yields a net *loss* at 4 percent.

The terrible effect of inflation and taxes works to erode your earnings. Because inflation occurs year after year and, just as inevitably, you have to pay taxes on your investment profits, you actually need to earn more than your assumed "good" profit just to hold onto your spending power. This problem leads some investors to the conclusion that they have to take greater market risks than they want, just to offset the losses caused by inflation and taxes. This, of course, has an undesired consequence. The higher the market risk you take, the more exposure to loss. So even with inflation and taxes in play, greater market risk than your level of risk tolerance will not solve the problem.

TABLE 6-1. BREAK-EVEN RATES

Effective	INFLATION RATE					
Tax Rate	1%	2%	3%	4%	5%	6%
14%	1.2%	2.3%	3.5%	4.7%	5.8%	7.0%
16%	1.2	2.4	3.6	4.8	6.0	7.1
18%	1.2	2.4	3.7	4.9	6.1	7.3
20%	1.3	2.5	3.8	5.0	6.3	7.5
22%	1.3	2.6	3.8	5.1	6.4	7.7
24%	1.3%	2.6%	3.9%	5.3%	6.6%	7.9%
26%	1.4	2.7	4.1	5.4	6.8	8.1
28%	1.4	2.8	4.2	5.6	6.9	8.3
30%	1.4	2.9	4.3	5.7	7.1	8.6
32%	1.5	2.9	4.4	5.9	7.4	8.8
34%	1.5%	3.0%	4.5%	6.1%	7.6%	9.1%
36%	1.6	3.1	4.7	6.3	7.8	9.4
38%	1.6	3.2	4.8	6.5	8.1	9.7
40%	1.7	3.3	5.0	6.7	8.3	10.0
42%	1.7	3.4	5.2	6.9	8.6	10.3

Other investors who consider themselves extremely conservative and risk-adverse choose "safe" but low-yielding investments. They may decide to invest their capital in insured certificates of deposit (CD) just to avoid market risk. For example, if your money is placed in a CD for one year and it yields 3 percent, what is your break-even point? If inflation is 3 percent and your effective tax rate is a very low 14 percent, you still need 3.5 percent just to break even. So the CD, in which you cannot withdraw money early without a prepayment penalty, is "safe" in the sense that its gross value (before inflation and taxes) cannot fall. But its true value will fall in many cases because of inflation and taxes.

There are some offsetting ways to reduce the effect of taxes, although inflation cannot be avoided. For example, if you set up a qualified retirement plan such as an IRA and invest through that account, taxes are not a consideration until you retire. In that case, you only need to beat inflation. So if you assume inflation is going to run at 3 percent, getting a 4 percent dividend on stock beats it, and a CD yielding 3 percent matches it with considerably low market risk.

A second consideration is the application of favorable tax rates, for both capital gains and dividends. You do not always pay a full effective tax rate on every kind of income; the application of a break-even rate should be tempered by actual rates as they apply, especially if a large share of your annual taxable income falls into those categories. You do not always pay a full effective tax rate on every kind of income; the application of a break-even rate should be tempered by actual rates as they apply, especially if a large share of your annual taxable income falls into those categories.

Liquidity Risk

You want to have your money available in case you need it quickly. The stock market is highly liquid and you can sell today and get your funds within three days. CDs are not liquid because early withdrawal causes penalties. Even less liquid than CDs is real estate. You can only get equity out of your house by selling, refinancing, or through lines of credit and all of these may take time and involve considerable costs.

It is not necessary to have all (or even most) of your portfolio in highly liquid accounts, for several reasons. First, you may have adequate liquidity with relatively small percentages of your overall capital. Second, the widespread use of credit cards lends a sort of temporary liquidity to personal budgets. For example, if you need cash next week for an unexpected repair to your car, you do not have to sell off stock. You can put the bill on a credit card and pay it off in one month, or if you prefer, over several months. Using lines of credit and credit cards is convenient and easy, and the only danger is becoming overextended. The point, though, is that traditional cautionary advice about liquidity is not always applicable. A few decades ago, before credit cards were in such common use, financial planners advised people to create emergency reserves equal to six months of income (more easily said than done) to ensure liquidity. Today, you can achieve the same safety net with two or three high-limit credit cards.

A problem associated with liquidity risk also involves the state of a secondary market. Past popularity of limited partnerships created problems because no secondary market existed; the only way to sell units of limited partnerships was to take deep discounts. This is unsatisfactory, but today you can invest in real estate investment trusts (REITs) and accomplish the same market advantages as real estate limited partnerships. At the same time, REIT shares trade on public exchanges just like shares of stock, so past liquidity problems can be eliminated altogether.

In an ironic twist, it is the high degree of liquidity that so often causes problems for investors. The stock market is liquid, but made even more so by the ease of access with Internet-based discount brokerages. The low cost of transacting business makes the market even more liquid, so today's stock market is much more accessible to the average investor than ever before. Only a few years ago, individuals preferred round-lot trading because the commission of odd-lot trading was simply too high. Today, that problem has been eliminated because execution is so automatic that there is practically no penalty for buying fewer than 100 shares. But in a way, this high liquidity can also cause problems. If it is too easy for people to make frequent trades, it is also possible to make more mistakes, or to make decisions at bad times. The low cost and ease of transaction presents a new twist on "liquidity risk," in which the higher liquidity itself creates a problem.

Another aspect of liquidity risk relates to margin investing. It is fairly easy for most people to use margin to double up on their investment capital. But this creates a new variation on risk, that of *leverage risk*. If you have $20,000 to invest but you are able to buy up to $40,000 in market value of stock, you could conceivably make twice the money, but you could also lose twice as much. Using margin to invest is a higher risk because you have to pay interest to your brokerage firm for borrowing those funds. Many people who would never consider borrowing money from a bank to invest in the market will go into margin without a second thought—even though it is the same thing.

▇ Nondiversification and Overdiversification Risk

Virtually every investor has heard about diversification; a detailed explanation and analysis of this topic is found in the next chapter. But in terms of the risk involved, there is always the problem of too little or too much. Your portfolio has to be diversified enough to reduce market risk, but not so much that you create a no-gain situation. With too little diversification, you are exposed to singular risks with too much capital. With too much risk, your expectations have to be lowered because exceptional gains will be offset by equal losses.

A lack of diversification is a problem, of course, and will be examined in greater detail in the next chapter. But what about the opposite problem, *excessive* diversification? Liquidity, always thought of as a positive attribute, can work against you in the modern market. Equally serious is the potential problem caused by overdiversifying. It is ironic. In the past, virtually everyone was aware of the need for diversification; today, you can diversify so effectively that you create a low-yielding portfolio than cannot outpace inflation and taxes.

In the modern environment of low-cost transactions and ease of accessibility to the stock market, diversification may become excessive. If you diversify too much, then your overall investment is likely to be mediocre. Exceptional gains will be offset by losses, so that overall you cannot outperform the market. This has been a chronic problem with mutual funds that grow so large they cannot offer exceptional yields. Even the relatively new exchange-traded funds (ETFs) are unlikely to outperform the market. By investing in a "basket of stocks" with similar attributes (same sector or same country, for example) you put your money into a broad range of issues. You would probably do as well or better by buying the leading stock picked by the ETF. For example, why buy every pharmaceutical stock offered through a pharmaceutical ETF when you could buy shares in the one or two companies with the strongest fundamentals?

Another problem is that without the need to buy round lots today, you can easily buy only 5–10 shares in a broad range of companies. Many will do well, many others will not. This overdiversification tends to have an offsetting effect, turning "excessive effectiveness" into ineffectiveness. Most proponents of the strategy known as *value investing* believe that you only need to own three or four stocks at the most, and that these should be the best-managed, bargain-priced companies you can find. If you can put your capital into shares of three or four companies and perform better than the market averages, it means you have just the right amount of diversification.

Lost Opportunity Risk

One kind of risk often overlooked is that of lost opportunity. This means that, if and when your capital is fully invested, you do not have any money available to take advantage of opportunities when they arise. Capital is usually finite and as long as your capital is already invested, the only ways you can seize new opportunities are to (1) sell something and move funds, or (2) borrow more money. Both of these alternatives are problematic because they may not serve your interests and may also bring additional risk into your portfolio.

Some investors unintentionally reduce their portfolios' liquidity when they take profits too early. For example, if you own shares of four companies and over time, two become profitable, should you sell? If you do, then your portfolio ends up with only those stocks that have either remained flat or lost value. Over time, by selling successful stocks and keeping losers, you tie up all of your capital in underperforming issues and make it impossible to jump in to new ones when you are presented with an exceptional value. You have no choice but to remain on the sidelines and watch your capital languish as the rest of the market passes you by.

It makes sense to manage capital so that some portion of cash is always available. Also, if you sell profitable stocks, you might want to sell paper-loss stocks at the same time. This accomplishes two things. First, it frees up more money by removing successful *and* unsuccessful holdings at the same time. Second, the capital gain in the successful company is offset by the capital loss in the other. This does not mean you should always take profits when they appear. It does mean you need to have a firm idea of when you will sell, based on price movement in either direction, to take profits *and* to cut losses.

The lost opportunity factor applies in other ways as well. For example, whenever your capital is fully invested, it limits your ability to remove money from your portfolio if it is needed for something else, like paying bills, for example. The only way to get funds out would be to sell stock you really would prefer to keep. You lose the opportunity for future growth by selling prematurely. Another point to remember: Investors sometimes time their buy and sell decisions based on dividend payment and ex-dividend dates. If you need to take the cash early, or if you don't have cash to make your move when you want, you lose that opportunity as well.

Finally, current news and changing events often creates exceptional bargains in the market. Because the market overreacts to all news, bargains come and go rapidly. A stock whose earnings are even slightly disappointing may lose several points of value in a single day. If you do not have cash available to invest and feel that the stock is going to rebound later this week, you will be unable to make a move. Being fully invested and having all of your money "at work" in the market might seem wise, but when you consider the range of lost opportunities, it is often an expensive strategy.

Some people deal with this problem by using margin investing if and when those momentary opportunities arise. But just as credit cards should be used sparingly for unexpected emergencies, margin investing should be used only in very exceptional cases, and always with full awareness of the risks involved. Lost opportunity is a problem, but overuse of leverage through use of the margin account can also be very high risk.

Margin investing, a fairly easy strategy to employ, can be quite risky. Exposure to profit opportunities always comes with exposure to greater risks. Using borrowed money requires that you make a greater profit than before because of the need to pay interest on the borrowed funds. If you are aware of the inflation and tax risk when you invest on margin, you have to overcome a *triple* stumbling block just to break even: inflation, taxes, and interest.

Because interest grows with time, you then face an additional hurdle with time working against you. Most stock investments benefit from time due to dividend income (especially if you reinvest dividends to compound your return), and well-managed companies grow over time so that the value of stock grows as well. But if you borrow money to invest in a higher number of shares, you face the problem of interest liability.

When you analyze the break-even demands of inflation and taxes, adding interest to the picture makes margin borrowing an extraordinary risk. In comparison, limiting yourself to available cash is more sensible, and for most people, a much more acceptable level of risk. You are better off missing some opportunities than you are by exposing yourself to higher risks by borrowing money to invest.

Risk management in your portfolio is a necessary feature. If you are not aware of the risk levels you face and of the various kinds of risk, then you cannot be aware of your own risk tolerance. It is important to set goals for when to cut losses or take profits. It is equally critical to decide in advance how much risk you can afford to take, what risks you have to avoid, and how to manage your risks to avoid unanticipated problems.

In the next chapter, the related question of diversification is expanded beyond the question of risk. Having too little or too much diversification in your portfolio will cause problems, but simply knowing how to diversify is an important attribute worth developing.

THE EGG-AND-
BASKET IDEA

D iversification is perhaps the most misunderstood concept in the
stock market. The most popular beliefs about being diversified is to
own shares of more than one stock, and it is considered "good"
diversification to invest in growth mutual funds. But these approaches do not always accomplish what investors need and want.

The approach of simply buying shares in a mutual fund is not
always adequate. For example, a fund whose management invests
with poor timing may experience losses greater than market averages in down conditions or perform below average in up conditions.
If you are fortunate and pick a good fund you can see great profits,
but there are no guarantees based on past performance.

Owning shares of stock in different companies is a good starting
point. It is equally important to be diversified in terms of market
sectors, and in some conditions investors should diversify outside
of the stock market as well, in the money market, bonds, or real
estate. The strategy of splitting capital among different markets is
usually referred to as *asset allocation*, a variation on the theme of
diversification. One problem with the allocation approach is a ten-

dency for "experts" to announce the best allocation model, and they expect everyone to accept it. For example, you may hear that this month an analyst is recommending 50 percent equities (stocks), 25 percent debt, and 25 percent cash. Does this *always* apply to you? Is it realistic to set up one model and assume that everyone should accept it?

Asking questions is a smart idea. An allocation model might be "right" for some people but not right for others, depending on personal risk tolerance levels and individual beliefs about the market. As with all forms of diversification, the allocation model should be established personally and based on what you want to achieve, what levels of risk you can tolerate, and where you believe profits are going to occur.

Investors concerned with the overall market need to study the question in greater detail rather than the simple assignment of percentages to various markets; in fact, for most people, allocation is set-up financial limitations. If you are buying your home, you already have an equity position in real estate. You probably also have some savings, so you are in the money market and have some built-in liquidity. Most of the rest of your money is likely to go into stocks or mutual funds. This is the logical level of allocation.

Within the stock market you need to be concerned about diversification between sector leaders and nonleaders. stocks that are interest rate sensitive and those that are not, sectors having differing characteristics in both market and economic terms, and stocks of companies of different status and longevity within their industries. Diversification is a form of risk management, and forms of diversification should take into account the profitability and prospects for future growth as expressed in terms of earnings trends.

Diversification Methods

To begin, consider the many ways you can diversify:

1. *By stock.* The most basic manner of diversifying is by stock. You simply buy shares in more than one company. However, buying

similar stocks (like different stocks in the same sector) is not going to diversify your portfolio effectively, because all of those companies will be subject to the same market and economic events.

You need to be concerned with how stocks are going to react to market-wide change. On those days when the Dow Jones Industrial Average (DJIA) drops 200 points, most stocks follow that course. Does this mean that all companies are inherently weak on the same day? Of course, it does not. But remember, the market overreacts to all news. When the 30 industrial stocks in the DJIA fall, the market tends to move in the same direction. It is equally probable that prices will return to previous levels within the next few trading sessions. The market should be viewed like a flock of birds, with every member of the flock moving and shifting direction based on whatever the leader does. There is very little room for individual thought in the flurry of the moment. But if you pick stocks with inherently good fundamentals, a strong competitive position, and a promising future the day-to-day price movement is not going to represent a permanent change.

Even so, picking stocks is risky. Just as stocks tend to follow the market leaders on the way down, they tend to do the same on the way up. This is the nature of a volatile market. Daily change is going to be extreme in uncertain times, but prices have a way of smoothing themselves out over the intermediate and long term. You accept the risk in exchange for the promise of future profits. But in picking individual stocks, it is wise to diversify by *beta* of the stock.

Beta is a technical indicator placing a relative value on how a stock's price moves relative to the overall market. The measurement is usually applied against the S&P 500 Index, which is a broader indicator than the DJIA. A stock that tracks the market exactly would have a beta of "1" and a stock that tends to move *more* than the market (meaning it is more volatile than the average stock) will have a beta above 1. Likewise, a stock that reacts to a lesser degree than the overall market (a very low-volatility stock) will have a beta under 1. An online search of "beta + stock" produces numerous sites for calculating beta and articles discussing this indicator.

2. *By sector.* It is more effective to buy different stocks in various sectors than to spread money around in the same sector. Real

diversification means more than avoiding "one basket" for your investment eggs. You also need to spread your money among dissimilar sectors. For example, buying three energy stocks is not effective, but putting equal amounts of capital in one each of energy, pharmaceutical, and utility companies is much more likely to spread your risks.

If you want to invest in a single industry, consider examining the exchange traded fund (ETF) market. One of the best sites online to look at the full range of the ETF market is on Yahoo! Finance at *http://finance.yahoo.com/etf.*

On the other hand, if you want to buy individual stocks but accomplish a sensible level of diversification, consider spreading your capital among sectors that are not going to react in the same way to the market. Study the economic and market features of the major sectors and identify how sectors tend to act and react to changing conditions, both market-wide and cyclically. Some sectors have predictable calendar-based cycles. Retail stocks are a good example. Other sectors, like utilities, are sensitive to interest rates. Defense stocks and oil stocks are more likely to react to emerging political situations and global conflict. In other words, each sector can be defined by its sensitivities. To diversify by sector, you need to pick sectors that are in favor with investors at the moment, but that tend to react to different sensitivities.

3. *By market.* The process of allocation among different markets further diversifies your risks. A very widespread market fall is likely to affect a broad range of stocks, so allocating your assets among stocks, real estate, and the money market (savings, certificates of deposit, etc.) is a wise move. Allocation is not necessary in all market conditions, however, because its importance changes with the market conditions.

It is important to realize, though, that diversification by market (allocation) is not always a matter of choice. For example, even if you believe real estate prices are going to rise in the future, how can you position your portfolio to take advantage of that change? You can buy property directly but that requires cash as well as effective cash management (not to mention dealing with tenants if rental property). As an alternative, you can buy shares in real estate investment trusts (REITs) or real estate development companies. However, this simply puts you back into the stock market in the real estate sector. In this example, an attempt to allocate only becomes an effective means for diversifying by sector, which might be enough. Additionally, if you are buying your own home, you have a duality of purpose. First and foremost, it is a long-term shelter for your family and that overrules investment decisions. Second, it is *also* a long-term investment. Based on price and down payment, you are not going to allocate less money in real estate unless you remove equity by additional mortgaging, which is often not a sound idea.

The same limitations apply to the liquidity issue. An advisor might suggest that you keep 25 percent of your portfolio in cash or savings, but that yields quite a low rate of return. Is it wise to follow this advice? As you have already seen, the effects of inflation and taxes create a floor of required break-even return. And the usual highly liquid, insured savings account or CD will not match it. If you are interested in the annual return, consider some high-yielding stocks and make your return via dividends rather than interest. Stocks are more liquid than CDs and have approximately the same liquidity as savings accounts but the yield is often far greater.

4. *By investment attribute.* You may achieve a more subtle type of diversification by spreading money around by *attribute.* For example, you might want to buy one high-dividend financial stock, one low-P/E energy stock, and one IT stock paying no dividend and with a high P/E. This diversification by attribute spreads risks while also exposing you to varying kinds of profit potential.

Attribute-based diversification, when structured along with an accompanying sector-based diversification, is very effective. Based on various kinds of market movement, for example, if your stocks all have low- or high-P/E ratios, the attribute itself may easily affect how the entire portfolio performs. While attribute differences might offset one another, it is often necessary to accept that limitation to protect your positions. For example, you might own three stocks, paying 5 percent, 3 percent, and zero percent dividends. The average of these three is 3 percent, so there is no specific yield-based advantage to spreading the dividend yield in this manner. However, the differences in attribute may achieve stronger diversification and protection of your capital.

Underdiversification

The most common problem among individual investors is lacking enough diversification. Many people believe that in order to be diversified, you need to own a broad array of stocks, and this is simply not true. Many people pick mutual funds primarily for the benefit of diversification, but this is not necessary. (A second reason often cited is the compound returns from reinvestment, but you can accomplish the same benefit with stocks by reinvesting dividends in additional partial shares.)

Having too little diversification may occur in many ways. For the most risk-sensitive person, mutual funds provide a sort of mega-diversification because these funds can spread money around in many stocks and sectors. The novice investor is likely to make three diversification-type mistakes:

1. *Simply having too little variety.* If you put all of your money into one stock, you are *not* diversified, no matter how promising the stock or how well positioned the company. Even owning two or three stocks that are subject to different market and economic cycles is often enough diversification. In fact, you can get enough diversification from three stocks, dispelling the myth that you have to buy shares of a mutual fund and be invested in 20 or 30 stocks.

For example, you would not achieve effective diversification by buying only energy stocks, utility stocks, or retail stocks. But owning shares of companies in all of these three industries is diversification. Energy stocks are sensitive to oil prices and political tensions. Utility stocks are most affected by changing interest rates. And retail stocks are annually quite cyclical but sensitive to consumer confidence and spending trends. These three completely different cycles and economic changes affect the three industries in different ways.

2. *Believing you are diversified when you are not.* Are you diversified if you own stock in three different companies? You might be, but you might not be. For example, if you own stock in three retail companies, you are not diversified, even with the subtle submarkets existing in every sector. Retail companies are affected by specific factors, and all are at the same overall risks.

It is also a problem to invest in three different companies with separate sectors, but subject to the same economic influences. For example, if you own a delivery service stock (like UPS or FedEx), a transportation stock (airline, trucking, rail), and a food chain stock (Kroger, Safeway), all are going to be directly affected by changing oil prices. They will be affected in different ways and to different degrees, but the lack of diversification makes this a potentially troubling form of selection. The likelihood is that if oil prices change dramatically, all of these industries will be affected in the same price direction, thus the approach lacks diversification. You would be more effectively diversified by identifying major influences on stock value and selecting companies in dissimilar industries. This way, when an outside factor (like oil prices) adversely affects one stock, it will not adversely affect the others.

3. *Applying personal bias so that the portfolio is placed at risk.* You might like real estate but fear stocks because someone you know lost a lot of money many years ago. For example, you might believe that stocks are excessively risky because your father or uncle placed the family savings in Enron in the year 2000 and lost it all. Remember that there are variations of risk in every market, and one experience can affect anyone's judgment. In the example cited, hindsight reveals that it was ill-advised to put too much capital into a single stock, whether Enron, Google, or Exxon-Mobil.

Personal bias can affect judgment about stocks, real estate, the money market, precious metals, options, commodities, or any other market. But it is often the case that the lack of a thorough understanding about unfamiliar markets causes a great deal of that bias. This bias also extends to brand names. For example, if you like the taste of Coca-Cola (KO) and do not like Pepsi (PEP), does that mean that Coke is a better investment? In fact, the differences in taste preference have absolutely nothing to do with the investment value of stock.

Some of the best-managed companies are also the most hated, not only for their high profile, but also for their simple success. High profile equals high target. Consider opinions you hear about Exxon-Mobil, Microsoft, and Wal-Mart. Many people detest these three companies, and yet, stockholders in all three have been amply rewarded. They are among the best-managed companies available. If you decide to *not* invest in these because of a social or political position, that may be a valid decision point, but be aware that the decision has nothing to do with *investment value*. If you avoid certain companies for noninvestment reasons like taste preference or social conscience, you should also be aware of the criteria on which that decision is made.

▨ Overdiversification

The opposite of too little diversification is too much. Some investors may be surprised to hear that such a thing even exists, but it does. The classic example is an extremely large mutual fund, so large that it cannot move in and out of positions quickly. These mega-funds hold so many publicly traded shares in their portfolio that their reasonably expected rate of return has to approximate the market, at best. All too often, even the large funds underperform because they are overdiversified. Table 7-1 summarizes the 10 largest mutual funds as of late 2007, as measured by net assets under management. Note that all are above $16 *billion*.

Mutual funds are not necessarily the answer to underdiversification. In fact, overdiversifying may be equally as damaging to your portfolio. Today, investors also like to select index funds or ETFs to cover entire sectors, types of stocks, or even countries. Remember that whenever you purchase shares in equity mutual funds, index funds, and ETFs your outcome will be equal to the average of all

TABLE 7-1. TEN LARGEST MUTUAL FUNDS

Fund Name	Net Assets (in Billions of Dollars)
American Funds Amcap A	$18.45
American Funds American Mutual A	17.46
American Funds EuroPacific Gr R5	17.24
American Funds Grth Fund of Amer R4	17.83
American Funds Smallcap World A	19.72
Fidelity Blue Chip Growth	18.89
Fidelity Dividend Growth	16.68
Franklin Income C	16.20
Lord Abbett Affiliated A	16.64
T. Rowe Price Mid-Cap Growth	17.29

Source: Yahoo! Finance, at http://screen.yahoo.com/funds.html

the components. For example, if you were to purchase shares of a pharmaceutical ETF, you would get a number of companies in that sector. Why not focus on the one or two best-performing stocks and receive a far better overall return? For the money invested, you would be smart to split among a diversified sector array than a single-sector ETF.

When you consider the size of some mutual funds—approaching $20 billion, for example—it makes sense to ask a critical question: How can such a large fund possibly beat the market? In fact, most do not. A study of a decade-long return comparing mutual funds to the S&P 500 was revealing. The average stock fund grew by 23.6 percent, so that $10,000 rose to $83,194 with reinvestment of income. That is impressive. However, the S&P 500 in the same period grew 28 percent, so that $10,000 increased to $118,074.[1]

Considering that broad diversification is a primary selling point for mutual fund investing, it is troubling that mutual funds, on average, did not beat the market. In fact, the average fell short by more than 4 percent over the decade studied.

You can effectively diversify within your own portfolio with a small number of carefully selected stocks. But the risk of overdiversification remains even if you limit your exposure. For example, some investors like to combine direct ownership of stocks along with a regular contribution to a mutual fund. The more capital allocated to the fund side of your portfolio under this incremental strategy, the more overdiversified you may become. Much of this depends on the kind of fund you pick, of course. No one would suggest that *all* mutual funds are overdiversified. But you expose yourself to this risk by purchasing shares of a fund, so it is sensible to consider the potential for a problem.

You can also overdiversify by buying relatively small numbers of shares in too many different companies and sectors. It should be adequate to pick a few leading sectors and buy the strongest candidates in each. This combination of factors evolves over time so periodic reviews are important, but by focusing on a relatively small number of sectors and stocks you are more likely to avoid the problems of overdiversification.

Bias and Diversification: Making Your Decisions

Another concern in developing a sensible level of diversification is that of personal bias. This was touched on earlier in the discussion of underdiversification, where the example of Exxon-Mobil, Wal-Mart, and Microsoft was used to make the point. These well-managed companies are also big targets for criticism from many groups. Social, union, political, and environmental interests all find fault with these companies, and it creates a specific bias against them. So why would you buy stock in any of these "evil" corporations?

The truth is that the bad press these companies have received is controversial, and is not believed universally. But even if you subscribe to the negative impressions of any company, should you avoid buying their stock? That is a serious question, because the shunning of a company's stock for nonfinancial and nonmarket reasons is a criterion outside of the usual.

It is wise to make decisions with your underlying premise clearly in mind. If you avoid a particular company because you believe that it pollutes the environment (Exxon-Mobil), does not use unionized labor (Wal-Mart), or crushes the competition (Microsoft), then you should be completely conscious of the reason. You may recognize that your own list of fundamental and technical indicators points strongly toward buying shares in these corporations, and yet you do not want to because of these biases. This is entirely legitimate, *as long as you know that this is why you make the decision*.

To expand on this, consider why and how some companies get a bad reputation. Many successful corporations are expected to contribute more than product at a competitive price, and this assumption can have unintended consequences. For example, in the case of Coca-Cola, which operates internationally, the following story appeared a few years ago:

> In October 2002, AIDS activists worldwide planned demonstrations and rallies to protest Coca-Cola, which they insisted must do more to help and treat HIV-infected workers and their families in Africa. Although the company had recently increased its benefits to provide anti-retroviral drugs to employees and spouses of its bottling companies in Africa, activists allege that the initiative will cover only 35 percent of Coke's bottler workforce in Africa and that its proposed 50 percent cost-sharing scheme will be too expensive for small- and medium-sized bottlers.[2]

This story is illustrative of the problem. The company had *increased* its benefits, but the criticism was that the increase did not cover enough of the local workforce. The question has to be asked: At what point does the cost/benefit ratio tip? If you were to take up the role of a social activist, you might want to avoid investing in Coca-Cola for the reasons cited. However, as an investor, your concerns would be quite different. What about the profit margin of the company's international unit? Is it the company's responsibility to reduce benefits to shareholders to provide extra benefits?

The question is often one of practical considerations, and not a matter of a cold desire for profits and lack of concern for human suffering. For example, the Wal-Mart debate involves two opposing ideas. First, the company provides thousands of jobs in communities it serves while offering lower prices. Wal-Mart's success is due to low prices. However, the major criticism of the company is that by not hiring unionized workers, it (1) underpays its employees, (2) exploits the poor, and (3) puts smaller local companies out of business. From the point of view of a person who needs a job, desires lower prices, and seeks a profitable investment, Wal-Mart's success model is apparent. The company has done well for good reasons. An individual who decides to not buy stock for the reasons cited should do so in full recognition of the difference in the decision-making model. You either buy stock in a company because it is well managed, competitive, profitable, and successful or because you approve of its operating model. For example, you might prefer shopping in a small local store where prices are far higher because you want to support local businesses and you don't want "big-box" stores in your community. But as a consumer you need to be willing to pay higher prices, and as an investor you need to acknowledge why you would not buy Wal-Mart stock.

Diversification is essential to protect your portfolio's positions. However, in attempting to create a healthy rainbow of variety to avoid suffering portfolio-wide losses, it is also important that you recognize your own biases. You need to determine your premise for investing in one group of companies versus another. However, most people will opt for better profits in the final analysis, according to a study done by the Wharton School. The study, "Investing in Socially Responsible Mutual Funds," covers the years 1963 to 2001 and found that:

> . . . funds that employ socially conscious criteria cost their investors 0.3 percent a month, which with compounding is actually 4.3 percentage points a year.
>
> The study lays the blame for the underperformance of socially responsible funds at two doors. One is that average annual expense ratios of these funds are substantially higher than those of others, about 1.3 percent a year compared with 1.1 percent. The authors assume these

costs result from the added research managers conduct to find companies they deem to be socially conscious.[3]

The study reveals that there may be a cost associated with socially conscious investing. The contention remains, however, one
between social conscience and the profit motive. As the author of
the above article pointed out, anyone who really believes in the importance of such an approach may adopt a different attitude: "I'd
prefer my mutual funds generate fat returns, leaving me plenty of
dough to contribute to charity, than sacrifice half my profits in the
name of so-called social responsibility."[4]

The danger of allowing personal bias to enter the analytical
realm of stock picking may also affect your ability to diversify. For
example, if you limit yourself to a specific range of corporations,
you may miss out on some very specific circles of profitability. For
example, if you believe that companies with substantial international
outlets "exploit foreign workers" and "move domestic jobs over-
seas," does that mean you should not invest in any international
companies? Some of the most successful U.S.-based corporations
are international in nature, and many attribute a majority of their
revenues to non-U.S. operations. In some cases, a specific bias, no
matter what the intention, could result in deflating your desire for
smart diversification.

Companies whose products and services conflict with your core
beliefs may surely be avoided, if only on the basis of personal beliefs
and opinions. However, it is also smart to be aware of the source of
the bias and how it may conflict with the typical investor's desire to
make a profit and to reduce losses. If your primary goal is to break
even after inflation and taxes, you already have a formidable task.
Limiting your potential investment realm further only works contrary to the sensible goals of a well-diversified portfolio.

In addition to the important personal management aspects related to diversification, your portfolio is also vulnerable to the issues
of *liquidity* in the market. This word has several meanings; the next
chapter focuses on portfolio liquidity, the need to keep your capital

at work but available at an appropriate level to generate profits and avoid losses.

Notes

1 Source: *http://www.atozinvestments.com/mutual-fund-return.html.*
2 *www.oneworld.net*, 10/17/2002
3 Timothy Middleton, "Feel-Good Investing? I'd Rather Make Money," August 19, 2003, at *msn money, http://moneycentral.msn.com.*
4 *Ibid.*

LIQUIDITY IN THE MARKET

"L iquidity" has several different meanings. In this chapter, portfolio liquidity is the primary topic of discussion, while other meanings of the term are also explained. The tendency among investors may be to take profits when they become available, thus, strongly performing stocks are sold off, leaving poorer performing stocks. Consistent application of this idea results in a portfolio full of underperforming stocks. This chapter explains how to avoid this and achieve the opposite: a portfolio full of exceptional performers.

Liquidity refers to management of a limited capital resource within the portfolio. Managing liquidity is an important function for every investor, and this function is tied closely to the identification of stocks by attribute (earnings per share, or EPS, as part of a trend, risk, diversification, and changes in trends in application of the Dow Theory).

The proper identification and timing of buy and sale decisions ensures that liquidity in the portfolio will not suffer. This is overlooked by many first-time investors and the more experienced investor as well.

Portfolio Liquidity: Available Cash

Portfolio management is far more difficult than people think. For some, it refers to the ability to pick stocks well, make consistent profits, and generate successful trades, meaning knowing not only what and when to buy but also when to sell.

The reality is far different than many perceive. It is considerably more difficult to time sales well and the tendency is to sell the wrong holdings at the wrong time. A related tendency is to hold onto stocks losing value, hoping they will rebound and fulfill the original belief that buying a particular stock was a good idea. Separating ego from human error is an important ability for investors. If you wait for your portfolio to prove that you were right in picking a losing stock, you are destined for future losses more than future profits. But if you are able to review your own performance pragmatically and with a view toward maintaining an expected return, you will probably see better performance in your portfolio.

This tendency—to sell profitable stocks to *take* profits and keep underperforming stocks to wait out a price decline—can be the most damaging practice to an individual portfolio. Your vulnerability is increased if, like most people, you own only three or four stocks at any one time. When one of three stocks is sold, that is one-third of your total. Will you replace it with another diversified stock or, like so many others, put the money back into stocks that create less portfolio diversification? When people take profits, it is very difficult for them to recognize the ongoing benefits of a company or even of a sector. The belief is that in taking profits and getting out, it is time to move on to other areas of the market. This is sometimes true, but based on a tendency to sell at the wrong time (for example, when prices are starting to move upward) it is a mistake to abandon a strong sector in favor of a weak sector.

The outcome is loss of portfolio liquidity. This assumes that the investor will continue to hold shares of underperforming stocks, and even worse, that upon taking profits the cash will be moved elsewhere. Thus, over time, this practice creates an underperforming portfolio. If you establish a rule that you will not sell stock unless or until you have a profitable position, this is inevitable: The lack of liquidity is self-imposed.

Consider the problems this flawed strategy creates:

1. *It is impossible to seize opportunities for future profits.* Profit opportunities come up suddenly, and it is always desirable to maintain enough liquidity to take advantage of some of them. You do not have to pursue each and every opportunity, just a few of them. For example, in an especially volatile market, the DJIA may fall 300 points or more. When that occurs, most stocks fall as well, even when their fundamental strength is unchanged. However, if a company is unfortunate enough to also have a disappointing earnings report on the very day the market falls, its stock may fall well beyond the level justified. That earnings report may be a slight disappointment. But remember, the market always overreacts and will take any bad news as a sign that at least for that company, the world is coming to an end. When this happens, a buying opportunity comes up. A stock that is pounded down to unreasonable levels is going to rebound just as strongly over the coming few days. It is simply the tendency of the market. So if you have enough cash on hand, you can buy shares when they fall excessively, even if that means you will sell at a profit in only a few days.

This is a classic opportunity, and the opposite of profit-taking. But there is another important difference. When the market surges upward and prices rise, you take profits but you then need to do something else with the money. The most likely action is to move that money to another stock that is also price inflated. This means that if and when the sudden price surge reverses, you will see a paper loss. In the case of a fallen stock price, you are able to buy shares at the bargain price and are also able to sell at a profit a few days later. So rather than being stuck with depreciated stock, you are faced with the timing issues surrounding appreciated stock. Most people would rather be in this position, of course.

The point worth remembering is that when you are fully invested and you have zero liquidity, you cannot look at the market objectively. You don't seek opportunities because you can't take them anyhow. You are continually worried about loss-position stocks in your portfolio, hoping their prices will rise, preferably sooner than later. You are like a person with very little money trying to shop for dinner. You can't afford the expensive cuts of meat or fine wine, so you end up in the frozen food section and the bargain-priced juice and soda section. You would *prefer* better food, but you can't afford it. This low liquidity applies in the stock market as well. If there is no cash available, you cannot even begin to think about the best way to manage your portfolio. Your only concern is what to do here and now to manage a bad situation.

2. *Simple movement of a small amount of capital is increasingly difficult.* The liquidity problem is not only limited to the inability to take opportunities. In such times, you cannot even afford to make relatively minor moves because you lose sight of your broader objectives and begin to think defensively. So if you have only a small amount of cash in your portfolio, it becomes more precious and you fail to take advantage of even small opportunities, such as a classic one-day price decline. You become overly concerned with making a bad decision and augmenting your problem, and perspective about the relatively small sums involved gets blown out of proportion.

Rather than continuing an effective method of portfolio management, investors in this situation go into "crisis management" mode. They stop thinking like investors. The alternative is to calmly assess the situation and develop some sound plans. For example, if you are approaching the end of the calendar year, it may be a good time to sell some stocks that have dropped in value and create a current-year tax loss. This is limited for federal taxes to $3,000 per year. You want to be sure that you don't exceed this level, because creating carryover losses is not efficient.

The creation of a tax loss mitigates the portfolio problem and makes the best of it in two ways. First, it reduces your tax burden while discounting the severity of the loss itself. Second, it gets those losing stocks out of your portfolio, which you need to do as part of the turnaround process. Every investor in this position eventually needs to "clean house" to get rid of the problems while changing the overall approach to the market. The tax loss is a good start. If you have had no capital gains this year, you can write off up to $3,000 in current-year losses. If you have previously had gains, you can sell even more. For example, if you have accumulated capital gains of $4,000 earlier this year, you can sell stocks and create as much as $7,000 in new capital losses, creating a net loss of $3,000 to write off. This not only gets stock out of your portfolio and frees up capital to invest elsewhere, it also eliminates the tax on your previously created profits.

3. *Poor performance tends to curtail future self-confidence.* Perhaps the most destructive consequence of low liquidity—especially when it is the result of underachieving stocks—is its effect on your self-confidence. Investors need to feel confident in taking the risks they are willing to take; when they begin questioning their own strategies, they lose the ability to take even acceptable risks, and inertia takes over. This destroys the person's ability to proceed.

What can you do when your portfolio value has dwindled, there is no cash, and all of your stocks are currently lower than original value? This is a troubling situation, but it can be solved. The long-term goal is to regain the initiative in developing situations in which you take losses in stride because you are creating profits that offset those losses.

Among the steps you can take is to consider a *new evaluation* of your strategic approach and risk level. You are either buying the wrong stocks, timing your decisions poorly, or taking too many risks. There is a tendency to try and offset past losses by getting more aggressive and taking on higher risks, but this may lead to even higher losses. Take a look at how you pick stocks and when you decide to buy. You might discover that you have become distracted, and this has created liquidity problems in your portfolio.

You can also reduce paper losses with an *option-based strategy* of portfolio management. This specialized market should never be used unless you first understand it thoroughly. Several strategies can be used to repair a damaged portfolio. First, you can write covered calls. In this strategy you sell a call (producing income) against 100 shares of stock in your portfolio. Be sure to structure the call so that if exercised, it will generate a net profit. The exercise price should be no lower than the net of your original purchase price minus the premium you get for selling the call. A second strategy is designed to protect paper profits. You can buy put on appreciated stock, so that in the event the stock's price falls, the put's value will rise to offset the loss. Finally, you can buy calls on stock when prices fall excessively. When the price rises, the call's value follows and those calls can be sold at a profit. Options are best used by conservative investors to *protect* portfolio positions or to take advantage of opportunities without having to (1) buy stock they don't want to keep, or (2) sell stock they would prefer to hold for the long term.

Creating Adequate Liquidity In Your Portfolio

In repairing a damaged portfolio, your goal is to mitigate the damage as much as possible and get out of poorly selected positions. When you have stock you no longer want, you are probably better off taking the loss and starting over with better-selected stocks. However, the creation of adequate liquidity should start with a critical examination of how things went wrong.

Examine your portfolio practices with these three questions:

1. *Do I pick stocks based on a short list of predetermined criteria?* Some investors create a sensible set of indicators by which to buy and sell stocks, only to forget to follow that list. In a highly volatile market with rumors of profit and fast-moving price changes, it is all too easy to become distracted by momentary speculative ideas, and end up taking risks beyond established and predetermined risk tolerance levels. It is crucial to (1) identify sensible stock selection indicators, (2) decide which indicators to rely upon to buy or sell, and most importantly, (3) ensure that you follow your own rules and resist the temptation to make decisions without analysis.

If you have wandered from this course, the first step is to evaluate the stocks you are holding and immediately sell any that violate your own risk tolerance standards. Taking a loss now is a better course than taking no action or hoping for the best. The first step in creating adequate liquidity is to get rid of underperforming stocks, starting with those that do not meet your previously established standards.

2. *Are these criteria effective in making good choices?* If you have been following your list of indicators but your portfolio under-performs anyhow, you have to figure out why. Is the market simply moving south at the moment and if so, do you think it will turn around in the near future? If the market is not in a decidedly down-ward spin, then what is wrong here? If your portfolio is not per-forming on a par with the market as a whole, you have to wonder whether your indicators are effective. Reevaluate your criteria with as much honesty as possible, and consider replacing any indicators that have not helped you to pick profitable stocks.

3. *Is my timing flawed? If so, how can I improve on this aspect?* You might be picking worthwhile companies to buy, but with poor timing. Do stocks come to your attention only when their price is rising? Do you consider buying after a price run-up while ignoring stocks that remain low or are even falling? It could be that this kind of selection process violates your otherwise well-picked indicators. When you only buy stocks whose prices have already risen, you may be buying at the price top of a short-term cycle. This invariably means that the price is going to drop after you buy shares, which is the opposite effect you hope to achieve.

In using your indicators effectively, you need to put price con-siderations at the bottom of the list. Prioritize your criteria to ensure that you pick companies that yield the desirable dividend, produce a long-term trend of growing revenues and profits, and are competi-tive within their industry. Then consider technical indicators like price volatility. The *last* criterion for picking a stock should be re-cent price action. In fact, if a stock's price has risen considerably over the last year and is now at or near its 52-week high, that could act as an indication that the opportunity was missed. Rather than taking the chance, you might be better off looking elsewhere. Even when all of your indicators work, the price history can disclose poor timing choices when you have mistakenly come to believe that the history of rising prices was a positive sign. By putting this test at the bottom of the list instead of at the top, you improve your timing.

A complete evaluation of the methods you use to decide whether to buy stock and then when to sell defines your effectiveness. You will need to set up liquidity practices in order to take control. For example, if you budget additional capital to put into your investment account each month, perform some personal asset allocation. Put a portion of that into a money market fund or a short-term CD (three months, for example, with staggered maturities). This creates immediate liquidity and allows you to grow more liquidity over time.

If you believe that the degree of liquidity can be best defined in terms of a percentage of your portfolio value, you should be putting that percentage of all new funds into a highly liquid account, and *not* using it all to immediately buy new shares of stock. You can also augment liquidity by moving dividend income from the investment account into a money market account. It is more desirable, of course, to reinvest dividends so that you get a compound rate of return, but that is not always possible. It is more important to create, build, and maintain liquidity as a first step. Only in this way can you regain the control needed within your portfolio.

Another Kind of Liquidity: The Market

Portfolio liquidity is essential and if you lack it, you need to take immediate steps to rebuild. You also need to evaluate how you make decisions and perhaps change some of your basic assumptions. Meanwhile, a different version of liquidity is always at work in the larger market, and it has a direct effect on the market's overall health.

Market liquidity is an economic indicator that determines how easily money is moved around. The market relies on adequate credit to pursue merger and acquisition (M&A) activity for institutional investors (mutual funds, pension plans, insurance companies) to buy and sell large blocks of shares, and for many sectors to operate effectively. For example, the home building sector—as everyone saw beginning in 2006—is as much affected by limited credit as by housing values. Financial stocks including banks, lenders, and secondary market organizations all rely on a healthy degree of liquidity (cash and credit), and when liquidity falls the market follows.

The simple ability to buy and sell stock, whether large investor or small, is a relative indicator of market strength or weakness. By definition, stocks are "liquid" because they can be bought or sold at current market for little cost; the transaction is completed swiftly and execution can be done at any time during open market hours. However, exceptions apply. For example, on days when trading is highly active you may experience difficulty getting through to your broker, so if you trade by telephone, high-volume days may create a disadvantage. High-volume days also create backlogs, so even if you execute trades online your execution could be delayed due to heavy volume.

Exchanges at times place trading curbs. For example, if the index prices move very rapidly in either direction, restrictions may be put in place to prevent runaway price movement. This rule was made after the very large market price drop on a single day in October 1987. Trading may also be halted for specific stocks in some cases. For example, if a merger is announced or some other news is released that is likely to create a lot of interest in a stock outside of the normal channels, trading can be halted for the remainder of a trading day.

Finally, market liquidity is subject to temporary changes due to exceptional events. For example, the New York Stock Exchange (NYSE) was closed for several days following the 9/11 attacks due to location as well as communications problems and priorities, not to mention the difficulty workers would have experienced getting to work in the Wall Street section of New York.

These exceptions aside, a liquid market is defined as one in which "ready and willing" buyers and sellers come together and agree on price levels for stocks. When prices fall, more buyers are available, and when prices rise, sellers tend to take profits. Price movement itself is a means for keeping up a level of interest, and its adjustment reflects ever-changing levels of supply and demand. Some markets are facilitated to ensure ongoing liquidity. For example, in the options market, there are times when buyers outnumber sellers (and vice versa). At those times, the Options Clearing Corporation (OCC) guarantees liquidity. It continuously acts as seller to all buyers, and as buyer to all sellers. As long as both sides match up, there is no need for facilitation. But in practice the OCC creates the other side of every transaction, and assigns trades based on tim-ing of placement and the need for its participation.

Concerns over market liquidity dominate the minds of bankers, Federal Reserve members, economists, and analysts whenever credit is tight. In 2007, for example, financial markets were greatly weakened by tight credit. The problems in the housing market were only part of the problem, affecting not only home builders but the banks and brokerage firms that funded mortgages, often aggres-sively. The weakened U.S. currency against other currencies, nota-bly the Euro, only made the perception worse.

From a financial market point of view, "liquidity" may include a subtle variation on meaning. For example, for a company that has financed billions of dollars in mortgages, market liquidity refers to the ability to transfer an asset into a different form *without losing value*. If a lender wants to transfer itself out of the debt it is carrying on its books in the form of mortgage loans, the ideal situation of liquidity enables the firm to sell off those assets near 100 percent value. But once perception—true or false—comes into the issue about unknown or hidden future foreclosures, that asset begins to lose value. At first, it can be sold only at discount. When the dis-count gets deeper, it might become impossible to transfer those mortgages. The unknown factor makes liquidity impossible. This problem, which often is far less severe than people think, carries a serious implication when it begins to affect investors. As one federal governor noted in a speech in 2007:

> Consider liquidity, then, in terms of investor confidence. Liquidity exists when investors are confident in their ability to transact and where risks are quantifiable. Moreover, liquidity exists when investors are creditwor-thy. When considered in terms of confidence, liquidity conditions can be assessed through the risk premiums on financial assets and the magnitude of capital flows. In general, high liquidity is generally accom-panied by low risk premiums. Investors' confidence in risk measures is greater when the perceived quantity and variance of risks are low.[1]

So, for example, if investors are deeply concerned about a fi-nancial company's *ability* to maintain its own profitability, the price of stock may slip. Even more to the point, when investors' perception is that there may be trouble ahead that the financial institution has not yet disclosed, the situation is made worse, even if the concerns are not true. Confidence is directly connected to risk, and market liquidity is a central theme you will hear again and again in terms of the financial and housing markets, interest rates, and consumer (investor) confidence measurements.

As the same federal governor observed in his speech, "liquidity is confidence." Investors, like most consumers, want financial certainty, or at least signs that future liquidity is going to be abundant.

Corporate Liquidity: A Fundamental Test

Most investors who study fundamental analysis know all about working capital tests like the current ratio. But what does this ratio actually reveal about corporate liquidity?

From the point of view of the corporation, "liquidity" is a measure of working capital. As a reality of business, companies must have enough cash on hand to (1) pay current expenses, (2) service debt, including interest as well as repayment, (3) expand the business as opportunities present themselves, (4) invest in essential capital assets, and (5) pay dividends. An examination of these primary liquidity demands demonstrates why management of working capital is essential:

1. *Pay current expenses.* The first and most basic demand on working capital is payment of current expenses. This includes payroll, rent, utilities, insurance, and all other necessary and *immediate* demands. A company that is chronically late in paying its bills faces some very real problems, and recovering from them gets more difficult as the problem worsens.

2. *Service debt, including interest as well as repayment.* It is too easy for corporations to slip into a spiral of debt. When liquidity is poor the temptation to borrow money is there, but this leads to higher future demands on liquidity.

3. *Expand the business as opportunities present themselves.* Expansion in business, as in nature, is essential to survival. Cash is the lifeblood of expansion, so companies like to move into new territories, expand product lines, and acquire smaller competitors. All of these activities require liquidity.

4. *Invest in essential capital assets.* Most big companies need to buy machinery and equipment, autos and trucks, and real estate. Few businesses can survive without investing in capital assets; many cannot grow and expand without those assets. It is not merely cash liquidity that is required to buy capital assets, but debt service liquidity as well. Many companies rely heavily on capital investment, and they need to plan ahead effectively to ensure that adequate cash will be on hand to repay borrowed money.

5. *Pay dividends.* Investors expect a return on their investment and there is natural competition between equity interests (stockholders) and debt interests (bondholders and other lenders). The higher the interest is on debt, the more difficult it is for the company to increase its dividend, or even to continue its current level of dividends declared. Annual increases in dividends declared is one important signal of growth in the business and its profitability. If a company acquires too much debt, it is very difficult to maintain long-term liquidity.

An evaluation of corporate liquidity should be performed on several levels. In Chapter 5, the important working capital tests of current ratio combined with debt ratio were examined. The point made there was that these two key ratios must be studied together. The example given was Eastman Kodak, whose current ratio remained steady over many years while the debt ratio exploded. This is a highly negative trend because the company acquired ever-higher debt levels. The appearance of healthy liquidity was deceptive.

Another way in which liquidity tests can be deceiving and even misleading is when companies carry large levels of inventory. This may cause the current ratio to decline over many years, even when conditions are actually very healthy. The need for increasing levels of inventory can distort the current ratio and as a result, exaggerate the condition of liquidity. Likewise, companies that do not carry inventory—those providing services rather than products, for example—should not be held to the same standards as dissimilar product-based companies.

For these reasons, two liquidity-specific variations of analysis should be applied. All liquidity tests are best performed in conjunction with a study of the debt ratio. In a well-managed company, the level of debt may rise, but the ratio of debt to total capitalization should remain approximately the same or decline over time. Slight rises in this ratio are acceptable when borrowed funds are used for expansion of markets, of course, but when debt levels rise over a decade from the mid-teens to 60 or 70 percent, it is clear that the health of the company and its liquidity are in jeopardy.

The first variation excludes inventory from the liquidity test. In companies with growing revenues and outlets, inventory levels may need to expand beyond the rate of growth in revenue and profits. As long as long-term debt levels remain under control, this is acceptable. Inventory growth may result in the current ratio's decline. An alternative is the *quick assets ratio,* also called the *acid test.* To compute a quick assets ratio, subtract inventory from current assets and divide the net by current liabilities. This formula is shown in Figure 8-1.

The standard for the quick assets ratio against which a specific case should be measured is "1 or better." The current ratio, you will recall, has the standard of "2 or better." An example: A company's current assets are $942,800 and inventory is $215,000. Current liabilities are $696,400. The current ratio and quick assets ratio are:

FIGURE 8.1. QUICK ASSETS RATIO

$$\frac{\text{current assets} - \text{inventory}}{\text{current liabilities}} = \text{ratio}$$

Current ratio:　　$942,800 ÷ $696,400 = 1.4
Quick assets ratio:　　($942,800 − $215,000) ÷ $696,400 = 1.0

Assuming that other fundamental tests, especially debt ratio, are in line with a long-term trend, the quick assets ratio is more meaningful as a test of liquidity in this instance. One of the problems of using this ratio, however, is the tendency for inventory to change seasonally. You can get a distorted view of liquidity if you apply the test at the wrong time of year. Some sectors, such as retail, have an unusually high-volume season. Retail companies often experience one-fourth of their total annual revenues and earnings in the last two months of the year. In applying the quick assets ratio, the same rule applies as with all liquidity tests. The ratio must be analyzed at the same time of the year and studied as part of a multiyear trend.

In applying liquidity tests to draw conclusions about the future growth of a company, it is also important to draw profitability into the test. In the ideal situation, a highly profitable and well-managed company will report annual growth in both revenue and earnings (especially as expressed via EPS), annual increases in dividends, steady ratios in working capital tests (either current or quick assets ratio), and steady or declining debt ratio.

Liquidity may, in fact, be as critical a test of corporate value as is profitability. You need both. But without liquidity today, profits tomorrow will decline or disappear, and that is the lesson. If you see debt levels rising, even profitable income statements cannot be continued indefinitely. Accompanying the fundamental tests of liquidity and profits, you cannot ignore *volatility*. Most people think of this in terms of stock price, which is clearly a valuable comparative technical test of risk. However, volatility is also a valuable fundamental test when applied to yearly financial trends. The next chapter takes a look at the many variations of volatility, and shows how you can use it to test a company's long-term value and safety.

Note

1 Kevin Warsh, member, Federal Reserve Board of Governors, speech at the Institute of International Bankers Annual Washington Conference, March 5, 2007.

VOLATILITY AND
LEVERAGE

T wo aspects of investing—volatility as a test of risk and leverage as the use of capital—are important tests of portfolio health and risk tolerance levels. This chapter explores these two aspects in depth.

Price history serves as the basis for many forms of market analysis, most notably charting. This chapter briefly describes the chartist's theories and ideas, and identifies the value of establishing support and resistance based on a stock's price history.

Volatility, which is one aspect of price history, is most often viewed only in one way—the volatility of the stock's market price. However, there are several problems with the most popular forms of volatility analysis. Spikes may be caused by many factors that will distort the typical analysis. Therefore, such exceptions should be removed from the analysis. The raw material for volatility analysis often distorts the picture. Studies of volatility are intended to provide investors with valid comparisons; this chapter shows how to adjust that raw material to make comparisons valid. The study of volatility helps to further differentiate companies whose fundamentals are otherwise similar or the same. Studies of volatility help to further define risk and opportunity.

Volatility tests risk, while *leverage* defines risk and profit opportunity in a different way. Most investors know the two most popular ways to invest: in stocks (equity) and in bonds (debt). A third way to invest is to leverage capital through borrowing money. Leverage is used when investors borrow through margin accounts, or when they use lines of credit secured by their homes.

The risk associated with leverage is significant because leverage requires higher rates of return. Because interest must be paid to borrow money, leverage requires special consideration. It usually does not belong in the typical portfolio.

All that being said, there is another way to leverage in the market. Investors may buy or sell options and by doing so, control shares of stock with minimal capital. This is also a form of leverage. In addition to comparing risk levels associated with options, the investor needs to select issues for option participation based on the fundamental trends of those companies. Thus, leverage cannot be viewed in isolation, but as an application of the ideas presented in the preceding chapters.

Analyzing Price in Terms of Market Risk

Investors tend to compartmentalize their analysis of stocks. As a result, the price at which they buy stocks is treated as a starting point, or a "zero value" price. The expectation is that from this starting point the price will rise. While such optimism is admirable, experience has shown that there is also a chance the price will fall.

A more enlightened view of price is that it is part of an ongoing struggle between buyers and sellers. This struggle, the essence of the supply and demand trend, defines how and why prices move. There are potentially infinite reasons for prices to change but for the combinations of all of those reasons, justified or not, the supply and demand feature in the stock market continues to define prices. And the more rapidly and broadly prices move, the greater the volatility for a particular stock. In its most basic action, the degree of volatility defines market risk. High-volatility stocks are less predict-able than the average, and as a result have greater market risk.

When you consider how supply and demand work, it makes a lot of sense. When many buyers want to buy stock, it drives up the price. As the price rises, it becomes increasingly likely that previous buyers will become sellers. As shareholders take their profits and sell, the demand ultimately weakens and falls away. This causes prices to fall. The further prices fall, the more attractive the price, bringing more buyers in to purchase shares at bargain prices. This action–reaction continues endlessly. The greater the change in price from day to day, the greater the volatility and market risk.

Another factor affecting volatility is short selling and short cov-ering. Short sellers sell stock as an opening transaction with the intent of closing the position with a buy order at a lower price. So instead of the traditional long sequence of buy–hold–sell, short sell-ers do the opposite: sell–hold–buy. The concept of selling some-thing you don't own is foreign to many people, but in the market it is commonplace.

Short selling is a high-risk strategy for two reasons. First, to sell stock short investors borrow shares from their brokers. The broker-age firm buys shares for the short seller and allows that short seller to sell them short. As a result, short sellers pay interest to the broker for the time their short positions are open. This adds to the need for a profit because the longer a short position remains open, the higher the interest cost. In addition, short sellers have to demonstrate that they have the financial means to cover their short sales if and when the transaction does not work out. Short sellers will profit if the stock's value falls, but if it rises they are required to increase their deposits with the brokerage firm. If the stock rises significantly, the requirement can become quite expensive. Based on financial capa-bility, most investors are going to be limited in how much short selling they can do.

The second reason that short selling contains high risks involves market price movement, especially in volatile stocks. If the price falls, the short position can be closed at a profit. But if the stock price rises, the short seller needs to cover the position, meaning

closing it at a profit or depositing more funds to satisfy the brokerage firm's risk.

Short selling can also be done "naked," meaning the transaction
is entered without borrowing stock from the brokerage firm. Conceivably, a speculator could sell a large number of shares without
any constraints, but the Securities and Exchange Commission
(SEC) limits this exposure, which was one of the contributing factors to the Crash of 1929. Regulation SHO is a regulation passed
by the SEC in January 2005 restricting short (SHO) sales, notably
naked short sales. This regulation limits potential losses due to
speculators being unable to deliver inflated price shares. This requires brokerages to close out positions within a short period of
time when speculators' positions have failed to deliver (i.e., they
have not met margin requirements).

Whether speculators borrow securities to go short or enter the
transaction naked, the widespread short selling of a stock can affect
its volatility. For example, when a stock's price has fallen dramatically, most short sellers close out their positions to take profits. For
example, if you sell short at $50 per share and the stock drops to
$42, you are likely to place a "buy-to-close" order and take your
money. When a lot of this activity occurs, it creates the illusion of
increased demand for the stock because a lot of buy orders appear
at the same time. Short selling can have an artificial, short-term
effect on the market, causing more traditional buyers to believe that
the buying activity is being caused not by short cover transactions,
but by permanent demand.

Volatility from shorting stock varies by the company and by the
overall number of shares involved. However, it is not really necessary to take such extraordinary risks when you believe a stock's
price is going to fall. A far less risky approach is to buy put options.
These options will increase in value as a stock's price falls. However,
options expire on their expiration dates, so there are risks involved.
For many investors worried by the risk of selling stock short, buying
puts is a low-cost alternative, even with its special risks. Another
alternative for anyone who owns short (other than selling when the
price has risen) is to sell a covered call. This specialized strategy is
more complex than many investors would like, and is only appro-

priate for those who have studied options and understand the risks involved. However, covered call writing is an exceptionally conservative option strategy. Option trading has become quite popular in recent years due to improved access to markets via the Internet and low-cost transaction fees through online discount brokers.

Charting the Trading Range: Quantifying Volatility

The causes of price volatility are complex and difficult to anticipate. In fact, anyone who studies market trends knows that the entire matter is quite unpredictable. But even those investors who rely primarily on fundamental indicators (usually the more conservative and traditional investors) can gain a lot of insight by understanding some charting basics. A few of the basic charting patterns are described and explained in Chapter 4. For now, it is important only to recognize a particular aspect of charting: the trading range.

The trading range is simply the space between the highest and lowest trading prices over a period of time. These boundaries are also described as resistance (the top price) and support (the bottom price). Resistance is the highest price at which sellers enter trades, whereas support is the floor, or the lowest price at which buyers will make their move. These aforementioned tendencies between buyers and sellers establish specific boundaries within "normal" trading. In highly volatile stocks you find a broad trading range, but in exceptionally volatile stocks the concept breaks down and trading patterns become erratic and unpredictable. In very safe, low-volatility stocks, the trading range is typically narrow and predictable.

The "ideal" trading range is moderate with a lot of price action within the range and no violations above resistance or below support. For long-term investors the ideal trading range remains constant, but the trend is upward. This means that the number of points within the range is constant, but the trend creeps upward consistently over time. Thus, a trading range and the existence of reliable resistance and support levels does not mean there is no price movement. It means the point difference is consistent even while price levels move.

The gradual change in pricing can occur in an upward or downward direction. A stock displaying moderate volatility can increase in value over many years or it can decline. High volatility is not the only threat to a stock's overall value as a long-term investment. Some companies have experienced deterioration in their price range over time, even when volatility levels have been low. The ultimate "value" of a company is not solely determined by its volatility. If you rely on long-term fundamental analysis of key factors (such as debt ratio, revenue/profits, and dividend trends, for example) combined with a study of volatility, the long-term action in price will be self-explanatory. Market price trends always follow the strength or weakness in the fundamentals.

For example, you can see how two stocks with relatively the same volatility levels have performed quite differently. Eastman Kodak and Wal-Mart are stark comparisons. Kodak, which was traditionally dominant in the film market, was very late to enter the digital camera revolution and actually resisted doing so for many years; they are paying the consequences more recently, both in fundamental and technical trends. Wal-Mart, the ultimate success story, has reported unrelenting and steady fundamental growth and its stock price reflects it. Table 9-1 summarizes these two companies and their 10-year trends.

The contrast is glaring. Before the well-known digital revolution in technology, Kodak paid good dividends and reported high profits, which reflected their market dominance in the stock price—at least for the four years early on in the 10-year summary. Since then, their fundamental and technical status declined. In comparison, Wal-Mart is a big success story. Profits have risen steadily as the debt ratio remains unchanged, and the dividend yield, while small, has grown consistently. It is no surprise that their stock price has followed suit.

This comparison makes the point about volatility. The trading ranges of these two stocks have not been that different, but one has shown a declining value while the other has grown during the same period. It is far too easy to conclude that "low volatility means low risk" and "high volatility means high risk." While there is some truth to this in technical and short-term trends, the longer-term in-

TABLE 9–1. FUNDAMENTAL AND TECHNICAL TRENDS

Company	Fiscal Year	Price Range	Net Profit ($ millions)	Debt Ratio	Dividends Per Share
Eastman Kodak	2006	$ 19–31	$ – 600	66%	$0.50
	2005	21–35	– 1,455	58	0.50
	2004	24–35	81	33	0.50
	2003	20–41	238	41	1.15
	2002	26–38	793	30	1.80
	2001	24–50	76	37	1.77
	2000	35–68	1,407	25	1.76
	1999	57–80	1,392	0	1.76
	1998	58–89	1,390	11	1.76
	1997	53–95	5	16	1.76

Company	Fiscal Year	Price Range	Net Profit ($ millions)	Debt Ratio	Dividends Per Share
Wal-Mart	2007	$ 42–52	$12,178	33%	$0.67
	2006	42–55	11,231	36	0.60
	2005	51–61	10,267	32	0.52
	2004	46–60	8,861	31	0.36
	2003	44–64	8,039	33	0.30
	2002	42–59	6,671	34	0.28
	2001	41–69	6,295	33	0.24
	2000	39–70	5,575	38	0.20
	1999	19–41	4,430	30	0.16
	1998	11–21	3,526	32	0.14

Source: Standard & Poor's Stock Reports

dicator is less reliable. Volatility cannot be used as the sole means for judging a company; you also need to track the fundamentals and determine whether the trend in overall value and strength is growing or diminishing.

Eliminating Spikes: The Need for Adjustment

Another important point to remember in any comparison among stocks is the fact that real-time price movement does not move in

predictable, straight lines. Short-term price change can be very chaotic, making analysis difficult. This is why the use of moving averages is so popular among technicians. Combining a 20-period and
200-period moving average is useful in predicting strength or weakness in current price, not to mention the likely future price trend
itself. If you use a 20-day chart, the 20-period moving average
equals the 20 days.

Because price movement is so erratic, it is important to ensure
that any study is made in a sensible and accurate manner. The widespread use of 52-week price ranges as tests of volatility is disturbing, because a simple point difference can mean vastly different
things. Some comparisons demonstrate that it is impossible to judge
all companies by the same standard. Exxon-Mobil, for example, reported a 52-week trading range near the end of November 2007, of
$69 to $95 per share. Based on the typical volatility formula, volatility for Exxon-Mobil was:

$$(\$95 - \$69) \div \$69 = 38\%$$

In comparison, McDonald's reported for the same period a
range between $41 and $60 per share, with volatility of:

$$(\$60 - \$41) \div \$41 = 46\%$$

How can you compare these two companies, given the similarity
in their ranges? Exxon-Mobil had a 26-point spread and McDonald's was 19 points, a fairly close trading range. The volatility is also
similar. However, Exxon-Mobil's daily price movement tended to
be more volatile (within its trading range) than McDonald's. Even
so, it's one-year volatility rating was lower. So the traditional
method is flawed. It would make more sense to apply a two-part
test to measure volatility. First, comparisons would be restricted to
the point spread within the 52-week range, and second, the test
should distinguish between rising and falling trends, or even trends
with little or no actual price change during the year.

Even high-volatility stocks cannot be accurately compared.
Google, which most people would agree is a very volatile stock, re-

ported a one-year trading range between $747 and $437, or 310 points. That is a lot of price movement. However, the stock's traditional volatility is only 71 percent:

$$(\$747 - \$437) \div \$437 = 71\%$$

This is described as "only" 71 percent in the belief that Google is far more volatile than some other stocks with lower prices and smaller trading ranges. In fact, Google's stock was so volatile that briefly, the price spiked to its high level and instantly retreated more than 50 points. This phenomenon—the *spike*—distorts outcome because it does not last. Google's trading range with the spike removed was actually between $690 and $437, making volatility look much different:

$$(\$690 - \$437) \div \$437 = 58\%$$

The difference between 71 percent and 58 percent is significant, even by Google's standards. If you remove the spike, volatility is closer to the acceptable "middle range" of stocks like McDonald's. This makes the case that even with adjustments to remove spikes, traditional volatility is inaccurate. The 310-point movement in Google, compared with the 19-point movement in McDonald's, hardly makes these stocks comparable in terms of real market risk or volatility.

Another problem with this traditional approach is that it does not make a distinction between stocks rising in value and those falling in value. Exxon-Mobil, McDonald's, and Google all rose substantially in the 52-week period ending November 2007. However, Citigroup reported a trading range between $57 and $30, only a 27-point change and hardly comparable to Google's 310 points:

$$(\$57 - \$30) \div \$30 = 90\%$$

This 90 percent volatility is quite high. But unlike Google, Citigroup's value fell during the period, with virtually all of that decline occurring between September and November. Thus, a true analysis of volatility would have to make a few important observations. First, the stock was very low volatility for nine months, reporting little actual change. The plummet in price occurred during a very brief period and reflected part of a market-wide credit problem aggravated by the subprime mortgage problems experienced by Citigroup and other financial institutions. Historically, Citigroup was never considered a volatile stock in terms of erratic trading range. The fact that the stock declined in comparison to other "volatile" stocks rising at the same time demonstrates the unreliability of volatility formulas.

To more accurately study volatility, a few important analytical observations should be included, such as:

1. Use the traditional test only as a starting point.

2. Study companies in terms of price trend rather than simple volatility. Some rise, some fall, and some remain unchanged.

3. Adjust the analysis by removing spikes. These are defined as exceptional price movements above or below a range when the price returns immediately to the previously established range.

4. Compare price point movement rather than percentages.

5. Be aware of the timing and extent of price movement as well as its underlying cause. Identify differences between market-wide strength or weakness versus changes in a company's fundamentals.

Leverage as a Form of Investing

Volatility in a stock is certainly a key indicator of market risk. However, you can also affect market risk in the way that you use capital. If you buy only when you have the full price of stock, you are acting in a prudent and conservative manner. The most popular form of market leverage, trading on margin, is high-risk and expensive. If price movement takes longer than you expect, or worse, moves in the wrong direction, your leveraged portfolio can easily lose value in a brief amount of time.

Leverage means using a specific amount of money to increase

your holdings. It is the third form of investing, after equity and debt. When you are an equity investor (stockholder), you have ownership in a company. When you are a debt investor (owner of bonds and other debt instruments like savings accounts, CDs, or shares of money market mutual funds), you have loaned money to someone else with the expectation of earning interest and getting all of your money back.

You can act as either equity or debt investor (or combine the two) by buying shares of mutual funds. An equity fund focuses on stock ownership, whereas an income fund tends to buy bonds that pay good interest rates. Balanced funds seek to provide both equity and debt, often with a focus on income from dividends on the equity side and interest on the debt side.

The third method, leverage, is based on the premise that by borrowing money you can increase your opportunities. This is a great idea in markets that rise quickly. If you have $10,000 and you borrow another $10,000 on margin, you put $20,000 to work. Even after paying interest, your higher level of equity holds out the promise for twice as much profit. But what if the market price of your stocks falls? In that case, your $20,000 portfolio may easily decline in value. If you had put the entire $20,000 in Countrywide (CFC) and Citigroup in August 2007, you might have lost one-third to one-half of your portfolio's value. Because $10,000 was borrowed to create the $20,000 portfolio, you could end up with a zero basis. If your portfolio's value fell to $10,000, you would have to repay the leveraged portion, leaving you with nothing. The potential return is twice as much with 50 percent leverage, but the potential loss is total:

Profit: $10,000 cash plus $10,000 margin = $20,000
         Profit of 50% = $10,000 gain
         Net outcome: Initial $10,000 at risk is doubled

Loss: $10,000 cash plus $10,000 margin = $20,000
         Loss of 50% = $10,000 loss
         Net outcome: Initial $10,000 at risk is wiped out

Leverage is beyond the risk tolerance of most people as a strategy, at least in its most popular form. Online brokerages make margin investing so easy that assuming too high a risk can occur without much effort at all. Anyone thinking only about the profit opportunities of leverage are wise to consider the risk element.

An alternative and safer form of leverage is found in the use of options. These enable you to control 100 shares of stock per option, but for only a fraction of the cost of the stock. For example, it is easy to find options for $60 stock for $600 or less. By buying options at $600 instead of 100 shares of stock at $6,000, you reduce your market risk and use leverage effectively. It is one of the few ways to employ leverage while *lowering* your market risk.

▪ Options as a Form of Effective, Low-Risk Leverage

Many people would like to leverage their capital but avoid doing so because of the risk. Borrowing money to invest is a bad idea for most people, so they limit their investment risk to cash they have available to place at risk. However, with options you can have the best of both approaches: low-risk leverage for a small amount of money.

Options are intangible contracts granting certain rights to their buyers. There are two kinds of options: calls and puts. A call grants you the right, but not the obligation, to buy 100 shares of a specific stock at a fixed price. A put is the opposite; it grants you the right, but not the obligation, to sell 100 shares of a specific stock at a fixed price.

Options expire at some time in the future. After expiration they are worthless, which is the major disadvantage of options. You need to realize profits before the expiration date, or you lose the money you spend to buy the option. In fact, 75 percent of all options expire worthless, so there are risks involved. Even so, there are many instances in which option plays make a lot of sense. If you are holding stock that has declined in value to a degree you consider unreasonable, you may buy more shares. But that requires putting more money into a stock whose value has fallen. Alternatively, you can buy calls. One call grants you the right to buy 100 shares of stock. For example, if the stock is currently selling at $30 per share, you could buy a 35 call (meaning the fixed price, or the "striking price," is $35 per share). If the stock rises above that level, you can buy 100 shares at $35 per share.

Most people who buy options don't actually exercise them, but sell them at a higher price than they paid. For example, let's say you bought a call with a striking price of $35 and the stock rose to $40. Assume you paid $200 for the call. Right before expiration, the call would be worth $500, because the stock is worth $40 per share but you can buy it for $35. Most people would sell the call and get $500 on their $200 investment rather than exercise. (If you wanted another 100 shares of stock, you would have the right to exercise and buy 100 shares at $35 per share; your basis would be $37, the cost of stock plus the payment you made to buy the call.)

Puts work in reverse. They increase in value as a stock's price falls. For example, if you buy a put when a stock is $50 per share and it falls to $45 before the put expires, it will be worth $500, again reflected in the difference between the stock's current value and the option's fixed striking price. Puts are very useful to anyone who owns stock. For example, if you have 100 shares of a stock whose value climbs, you may be tempted to take profits, fearing the price will retreat. But if you prefer to continue holding the stock, you could buy a put instead. This is a form of insurance. If the stock's value falls, then the put will increase in value, offsetting your paper loss.

These examples of calls and puts protect portfolio positions without requiring you to put additional capital into depreciated stock, or take profits when you would rather continue holding the stock. In this application of calls and puts, they are excellent portfolio management tools. And if you invest $200 and sell for $500, that is a 250 percent return! It is even possible to realize such returns very quickly if and when a stock's price moves. However, offsetting this is a reality: If the stock does not move in the desired direction, the loss of an option is likely to be 100 percent. As dire as that sounds, remember that the cost of the option is quite low, commonly less than 10 percent of owning shares. (The actual cost depends on the time left until expiration and the proximity between the striking price and current market value.) The leverage is valuable, given the limited capital requirements. You may hesitate to invest as much as $5,000 for a $50 stock but you can have the same control as a stockholder for only a few hundred dollars. If the price changes in the direction you anticipate, your return is also leveraged.

For example, you can buy 100 shares of a $50 stock and pay $5,000, or buy a call for $500. If the stock moves up $2\frac{1}{2}$ points, the outcome between stock and option is quite different upon sale:

Stock: $250 ÷ $5,000 = 5%
Option: $250 ÷ $500 = 50%

You leverage capital with options in the capital requirement itself. For example, if you have $5,000 to invest, you can buy 100 shares of a $50 stock or 200 shares of a $25 stock. Or, you can buy 10 options at $500 each or 20 at $250 each. You could even spread your capital among many different stocks. For conservative investors, this is not necessarily a prudent approach, remembering that 75 percent of options expire worthless. However, it makes the point that options are valuable supplementary tools for managing a portfolio, especially in volatile markets.

The fact that 75 percent of all options expire worthless points to a different approach of making options even more valuable. You can *sell* options, which places you on the other side of the transaction. Just as short sellers of stock can sell shares they do not own, option sellers can also sell options. Of course, simply selling an option would be considered very high risk by itself. But if you own 100 shares of stock, you can sell (or as it is called, write) a covered call. This means that if the stock's value rises above the striking price, the call will be exercised and your 100 shares will be called away at the fixed striking price.

For example, if you bought 100 shares of stock at $30 per share and the stock has been selling recently around $40, you can write a covered call with a striking price of $40. This means that if the stock rises higher, the option will be exercised and your stock will no longer belong to you. Upon exercise, you will get $4,000 for your 100 shares. Even if the stock's value rises to $60 or $70, exercise always occurs at the striking price.

Given the reality that most options expire worthless, the chances of exercise are small. It happens, but not every time. This strategy would make sense based on your original purchase price, so that in the event of exercise you make a profit on the stock. In this example, you would make $1,000 (purchase price of $30, exercise price of $40). In addition, you keep the option premium and any dividends earned before exercise. In the entire history of ownership of this stock, for example, you would earn the following (assuming option value at time of writing the covered call of $400, dividend yield of 3 percent based on $30 per share, a holding period of exactly one year, and not including transaction costs):

Exercise price of stock	$4,000
Less: original cost	− 3,000
Profit on stock	$1,000
Sale of covered call	400
Dividend, 3%	90
Total profit	$1,490

Based on the original investment of $3,000, this $1,490 return represents overall profit of 49.7 percent—not bad for a one-year history. This is the "return if exercised" calculation including all forms of income: capital gain, option, and dividend. However, given the reality that most options expire worthless, the outcome is quite different. Considering the option by itself and assuming it expired worthless, the return would be:

$$\$400 \div \$3,000 = 13.3\%$$

The original basis of stock is used based on the rationale that the covered call is made possible by the investment in the stock and its basis is $30 per share. Some would argue that the calculation is more accurately based on the striking price of $40 per share:

$$\$400 \div \$4,000 = 10.0\%$$

In either case, the return is impressive. It is also worthwhile to note that after selling a covered call and waiting until expiration, you are able to repeat the process. You can sell covered calls indefinitely. There are three possible outcomes. First is exercise, second is expiration, and third is closing out the call at a profit. For example, if you sell the covered call for $400 and it is later worth only $150, you can enter a "buy-to-close" transaction and close out the position. In this transaction, your profit would be $250.

All three outcomes are impressive and relatively safe. The only real risk you face is the risk that the stock rises far above striking price and you give up shares below current market value. Most people will gladly accept that risk and the occasional lost opportunity in exchange for the certainty of double-digit returns every year.

Options point out the reality that there are alternatives to simply buying and selling shares of stock. A sophisticated approach recognizes the value of using options in several ways: as tools for pure price speculation in volatile markets; protection of paper profits; taking advantage of exceptional price declines; and of course, covered calls. There are many other ways to invest in the market without actually buying shares of stock. The next chapter explores some of these alternatives.

ALTERNATIVES TO DIRECT OWNERSHIP OF STOCKS

There are many ways to own or control stocks beyond direct ownership of shares. The popularity of mutual funds cannot be ignored, as these enable diversification by sector or between stocks and bonds. The newer form of mutual fund, the exchange-traded fund (ETF), helps investors to further diversify a portfolio and still enjoy liquidity by trading shares on the exchanges just like stocks.

Mutual fund fees can be complex because they come in many forms, some of which are hidden. This makes comparison difficult. This chapter provides guidelines for making valid comparisons between funds. Other investment alternatives include trading in index funds on the market where profits are earned if and when a market index rises, or placing funds into sector ETFs.

The options market also enables investors to control shares of stock for only a fraction of the cost of buying shares. The potential profits and risks of options are also explained in this chapter.

■ The Mutual Fund Alternative

Mutual funds are vastly popular for many reasons, including low cost, historical performance, and convenience. When you place money in a mutual fund, you allow professional management to make decisions about which stocks to buy or sell. The fund itself is a *conduit* investment, meaning profits or losses are passed on to individual shareholders. The mutual fund company is a conduit between the market and investors. The fund itself does not accumulate profits or losses other than the compensation paid to its professional management.

Making comparisons between different mutual funds is difficult. The most popular way that one fund is picked over another is on the basis of past performance. But as the disclosure warns, "past performance is no indication of future performance." So a fund that outperformed the market last year might do poorly this year, and vice versa. When looking at performance as a method for picking a fund, you may want to also focus on funds that did well when markets fell, and not only those that succeeded as markets rose.

Another means for comparison is size, measured in dollar value of assets under management. An exceptionally small fund may offer a lot of growth potential, and a fund that limits the amount of dollars it accepts from investors may be more easily managed in the future. In comparison, funds that have grown to exceptionally high asset levels may have difficulty in moving money around quickly in changing markets. These funds tend to invest broadly, so out of necessity their profit or loss is going to approximate the overall market, at best.

Fund comparisons are further complicated by the fees they charge, and fee structures are not always comparable. Before you determine in which funds to invest, always read the prospectus and pay special attention to the section called "Shareholder Fees," where funds are required to explain all of their fees and charges. Any side-by-side comparison is complicated because fee structures vary so widely. Some fees to be aware of:

1. *Sales load* is applicable when you buy fund shares through a broker or financial planner. The sales load, also called sales charge

load, is a commission you pay to the broker. The load usually is 8.5 percent, although funds may charge less. The problem with sales load is that it comes off the top. For every $100 you invest (assuming maximum load), $8.50 goes to a salesperson's commission and only $91.50 goes into the investment. So in a fund not charging a sales load, a 5 percent return represents $5.00 per $100. But to make that $105 in a load fund you have to earn 14.75 percent, nearly three times more.

$$\$105.00 - \$91.50 = \$13.50$$
$$\$13.50 \div \$91.50 = 14.75\%$$

The sales load makes a significant difference in matching no-load fund returns. However, in studies comparing load and no-load funds, market performance is no different. To justify the sales load, commission-based advisers claim that their expertise in fund selection is worth the commission they are paid; but realistically, few financial planners undertake the comparisons needed to make such claims.

In addition to the "front-end sales load" described above (in which the commission is deducted before money is even placed in the investment), some funds charge a "back-end sales load," also called a deferred sales load. This is paid when you redeem your shares, so the commission comes out of accumulated funds rather than off the top. The most frequently used type is called the contingent deferred sales load, or CDSL. The amount charged depends on how long you hold onto your shares. The load fee declines for each year you keep your fund shares, eventually falling to zero.

Some mutual funds advertise that they are "no-load," implying that investors will not be charged a fee. But here again, careful comparisons of the full range of fees is essential, because even a no-load fund might assess additional fees given names like purchase fees, redemption fees, exchange fees, or account fees. None of these are classified as a "sales load," and as long as the combination of all extra fees does not exceed 0.25 percent of the fund's net asset value, the fund is still allowed to call itself a no-load fund.

2. Yet another charge is the *redemption fee*, which is charged whenever investors sell (redeem) their shares, in total or a portion of the total. This is not treated as a sales load by name, even though it is deducted in the same manner as a back-end sales load. But whereas a back-end sales load goes to a broker or financial planner, the redemption fee is ostensibly assessed for costs the fund has to pay for the redemption. The limit of redemption fees is 2 percent under Securities and Exchange Commission (SEC) guidelines.

3. *Other fees*: Mutual funds have cleverly defined and crafted their fee structures to avoid calling them sales load or expense fees. An *exchange fee* is assessed by some mutual funds if and when investors transfer funds to another fund within the same group, or "family" of funds. An *account fee* is charged to maintain an account in some cases, which is increasingly difficult to justify in an automated age. The account fee often is assessed on accounts whose value falls below a specified dollar amount. A *purchase fee* is charged when you buy shares. Not called a sales load but assessed in the same way, the money goes to the fund rather than to a broker.

4. *Operating expense fees* are charged by virtually all mutual funds and come in a variety of forms. The *management fee* is the fee paid out of the fund's asset to compensate its professional managers, and an *administrative fee* is paid to an investment adviser. Each shareholder is assessed an annual portion of the overall fee paid.

5. Some funds also charge a *12b-1 fee*, named for the SEC rule authorizing these special charges. It is also called a "distribution fee," and covers the costs of paying for advertising and marketing the fund's shares. This includes placing actual ads as well as printing and mailing prospectuses and marketing and sales literature. The maximum 12b-1 charge per year cannot exceed 0.75 percent of average net assets per year, under the rules of the National Association of Securities Dealers (NASD). Essentially, a 12b-1 fee requires its investors to pay the cost of advertising the fund and attracting more investors. Some plans include a secondary *shareholder service fee*, which covers the cost of responding to investor inquiries. Some funds charge this shareholder service fee without

calling it a 12b-1 fee. The maximum is 0.25 percent per year under NASD rules.

6. *Other expenses* can also be charged by funds. In addition to the fees listed above, these may include custodial expenses, legal and accounting expenses, transfer agent expenses, and administrative expenses.

As you can see, an array of fees may be disclosed or hidden in the fine print of a prospectus, a document most people don't read. Many people limit their selection to no-load funds only—those that do not assess a load fee—but may actually be paying a range of fees without even being aware of them. The monthly or annual statements issued by funds can be very difficult to read, and many investors do not know how to find the total of all the fees they are paying. The fee table in the prospectus includes the "total annual fund operating expenses," which is the fund's annual operating expenses, expressed as a percentage of average net assets.

However, it remains true that comparing fees between funds is very difficult, given the variety of fee names and structure of the fees themselves. And on the basis of performance, the net outcome makes the comparison even more difficult. For example, when you hear that a fund's 10-year return to investors was 10 percent, what does that mean? Is this based on returns before or after expenses? How does that fund compare to other funds charging more fees or fewer fees?

Finding Help in Making Comparisons: The best way to make valid comparisons between different funds is to undergo a side-by-side comparison with all fees included. A "mutual fund expenses analyzer" is free and located at *http://apps.finra.org/Investor_Information/EA/1/mfetf.aspx*. Another one, offered free on the SEC Web site, is located at *http://www.sec.gov/investor/tools/mfcc/holding-period.htm*.

In addition to the web of fees mutual funds charge, another method for judging and comparing them is through analysis of their *net asset value (NAV)*. This is the current market value of all assets, minus liabilities, divided by the total shares of the fund. You can find NAV in daily listings in financial papers or investment sites online. Most funds are referred to as open-end funds, meaning they will accept an unlimited number of additional investors and do not impose a limit. A closed-end fund, in comparison, has a specific dollar value limit, and when closed will not accept any new investors (however, in many such funds, existing investors are allowed to buy additional shares). Shares can be purchased by new investors only on the exchanges, and only when they are offered by existing investors, rather than simply sold by the fund itself. In an open-end fund, the NAV reflects specific net market value of the portfolio minus what the fund owes to others. But in a closed-end fund, NAV might trade above the tangible value of the company. When shares are valued at a premium above actual tangible value, it implies that investors perceive growth potential in the future based on the fund's portfolio and its management.

Classifications of Funds

In addition to distinguishing funds by fee structure, you need to decide which type of fund you want. This distinction should be based on the types of investments included in the fund's portfolio, as well as its investment objectives.

Types of funds include the following:

1. *Equity funds* invest in stocks and take equity positions in listed companies. As "institutional" investors, equity funds often purchase large blocks of stock rather than only a few hundred shares. Because the majority of dollar value in the market is represented by institutional holdings and trades, large institutions (mutual funds, insurance companies, and pension funds, for example) have a lot of influence on price movement in specific stocks.

2. *Fixed income funds* invest in two kinds of securities. They buy bonds to generate interest income for investors and a limited amount of capital gains. For example, when bonds are sold in the market at a discount (meaning below their face value), they are re-

deemed at full par value; the difference is a capital gain. An income fund may also invest in equity positions to generate dividends. Some fixed income funds, also called bond funds, may also specialize. For example, they may invest only in high-yielding bonds (junk bonds) that while yielding higher than market rates also represent greater market risks.

3. A *money market fund* limits its investments to the money market, including certificates of deposit and other short-term, interest-bearing instruments. These include instruments like U.S. Treasury bills, bankers' acceptance, and commercial paper. These kinds of instruments represent the cost of banks and other institutions lending money to each other or providing financial guarantees in very short periods of time. Funds specializing in this market carry portfolios of various money market instruments and pay interest to shareholders.

4. A *specialty fund* can be designed to emphasize equity, debt, or money market instruments, but has a specific kind of distinction beyond the broader classifications. For example, a fund may specialize in new, fast-growing companies, a specific market sector, a country or region, or even environmentally conscious companies (so-called "green" funds). Specialization may come in a variety of forms, often designed to hedge against currency or precious metal weakness in one country, or to take advantage of emerging economic conditions internationally. Even greater specialization is found in mutual funds with very narrow investment criteria. For example, *global funds* (also called international funds or foreign funds) focus primarily on companies outside of the United States.

5. *Balanced funds* provide investors with a combination of features on two levels.

First is market risk versus safety; in other words, a balance exists between potential income and growth on one hand versus safety of capital on the other. The balance may also refer to the use of different kinds of instruments and may be called an asset allocation balance fund. A portion is invested in stocks and a portion in bonds, and may be more finely distinguished by the type of stocks employed. For example, some portion may be allocated to financial markets or real estate company stocks, creating allocation between stocks, real estate, and debt.

6. Another way to define and distinguish mutual funds is by the asset value of companies in their portfolios. A *large-cap fund* limits itself to stocks of companies with very strong financial value, meaning a conservative rate of return and lower than average chances of large-scale losses in stock value. In comparison, *mid-cap* and *small-cap funds* select companies with less capital value but greater growth potential.

7. *Index funds* invest in a cross-section of stocks found in specific market indices such as the S&P 500 or Dow Jones Industrial Average (DJIA). For example, buying shares in a DJIA index fund would provide investors with a portion of ownership in all 30 stocks on the DJIA, and buying shares in an S&P 500 mutual fund would give ownership proportional shares in all 500 of those companies. Logically, it would seem prudent to limit investment to the top performing companies in an index, and some specialized mutual funds do just that. Investors who opt for index mutual funds want the broad exposure without the diversification and management problems involved with buying shares of many companies; the index fund provides an easy and affordable solution.

8. *Tax-free bond funds* are suitable for those paying very high tax rates. Some bonds, specifically municipal bonds, are exempt from income taxes. In analyzing a bond fund a valid comparison should be made on an after-tax basis. In other words, the tax-free income from a bond fund has to be compared to the income from a taxable mutual fund after taxes are paid.

Fund selection should also be made on the basis of investment objective and financial status. For example, you would not want a lower-yielding tax-free bond fund if your tax rate is low. A *growth fund* is designed to emphasize investment in companies expected to have exceptional growth in the future. This is designed to provide greater than average capital gains. A *value fund* seeks stocks that can be bought at a discount but are exceptionally well managed and expected to produce higher than average returns over many years.

An *income fund* focuses on higher than average dividend yields, often including limitation to stocks whose dividends have grown every year over many years (dividend achievers).

A fund promising to focus on *capital preservation* seeks investments that will beat inflation and taxes, but will not take any risks that would lead to substantial market value decline. On the other side of the risk spectrum, an *aggressive growth fund* is like the middle-of-the-road growth fund, but seeks much greater than average growth. The investment objective is just that and not a promise of future performance, an important point to keep in mind. Mutual funds as a group have not outperformed market averages for the most part in past years, and finding the fund that is likely to outperform future markets is no easy task. It makes the most sense to focus on funds that have shown consistent performance in many different types of market conditions, and whose management communicates a specific, prudent investing policy with a proven track record.

Other Conduit-Type Investments

Beyond the traditional mutual fund, a number of more specialized conduit investments offer an alternative to direct ownership of stocks.

Among these, the *mortgage pool* offers investments in secured real estate mortgages. These are marketed by quasi-government agencies, which collectively are referred to as the real estate's *secondary market*. These mortgage-backed securities are derived from the mortgage market itself. Lenders underwrite loans to homeowners, for example, and then sell those loans on the secondary market. Mortgages are packaged together and sold to investors. Different forms of these mortgage pools are offered by the Government National Mortgage Association (GNMA), also known as "Ginnie Mae" (*www.ginniemae.gov*), which sells an instrument called the Real Estate Mortgage Investment Conduit (REMIC); by the Federal National Mortgage Association (FNMA), or "Fannie Mae" (*www.fanniemae.com*), which offers REMICs and "mega-pool" investments; and by the Federal Home Loan Mortgage Corporation (FHLMC), or "Freddie Mac" (*www.freddiemac.com*), which also sells REMIC products. A variety of other organizations also offer mortgage-backed and mortgage-debt securities.

Another alternative to direct ownership involving real estate is the real estate investment trust (REIT). A useful Web site providing an industry overview is the National Association of Real Estate Investment Trusts (NAREIT) at *http://nareit*.org. REIT shares sell just like shares of stock on public exchanges, making these among the few real estate investments with good liquidity. Many offer dividend reinvestment options, so you can choose to receive dividends in additional partial shares instead of cash. This creates a compound return on the REIT shares. REITs are specialized in the way they invest. An *equity REIT* is designed to buy property directly, usually without carrying any debt. Thus, returns from rents are higher than they would be if it were necessary to pay interest on a mortgage. A *mortgage REIT* specializes in lending money to developers and builders. A *hybrid REIT* combines equity and mortgage features, taking up equity as well as debt positions. Most REITs specialize by type of property. For example, some buy only industrial parks, whereas others focus on multifamily residential or commercial properties. Another pooled investment is the limited partnership. In this real estate company, investors buy units of interest and general partners manage the company, picking properties and deciding when to hold or sell. There are several disadvantages to limited partnerships. First, you are "limited" in the sense that you have no say over how the funds are managed. Second, if there are tax losses they are classified as "passive losses," and cannot be claimed but must be saved and applied against future "passive gains." Third, when you want to sell limited partnership units, the secondary market value is not always based on actual value; the only way out is to sell units at a discount, often a deep discount, to companies set up specifically to buy "used" shares of limited partnerships. For most investors, limited partnerships offer little value compared to other investment alternatives.

Investing in real estate, which is often very illiquid, is most easily accomplished through REIT or other conduit venues. But for anyone seeking a lot of flexibility, whether in real estate, stocks, currency investments, or specific sectors, one kind of mutual fund—the ETF—is especially designed for low cost and diversification.

Exchange-Traded Funds

An exchange-traded fund, or ETF, is a variation on the more traditional model of a mutual fund with some important differences. The portfolio of a traditional fund varies as management makes decisions, buying new issues and selling old ones. An ETF has a portfolio with a basket of stocks that is identified in advance and does not change.

A second important difference is that ETF shares are bought and sold on the exchanges just like stocks. To buy or sell traditional mutual fund shares you have to work directly with the fund, and that invariably means extra costs will be assessed and the transaction will take time. Many ETFs also allow investors to transact options on their basket of stocks, which opens up many possibilities beyond simply owning shares of the fund.

Because there is no actual management of an ETF once its basket of stocks has been defined, the costs of ETF investment are far lower as well. Of course, certain expenses will be charged and even with no actual management decisions, the ETF still has to be managed and expenses will apply, but these expenses are far lower than those in traditional mutual funds.

Trading ETF shares is flexible as well. You can buy or sell at any time during the hours the stock exchange is open. The less flexible traditional mutual funds are always bought and sold based on value at the end of each day. However, this is not always a benefit. ETFs don't always trade at their net asset value (NAV), but could trade above or below the market value of the ETF holdings. In other words, ETF pricing is more like that of a stock and nothing like traditional mutual funds.

Beyond ETFs for stocks, an additional alternative is the ETN, or exchange-traded note. Many people find bonds attractive but cannot afford the cost of trading in individual notes or the high commissions of some bond funds. In an ETN, a basket of debt securities (notes, bonds, money market instruments) is made available with terms similar to the ETFs in the stock market.

Getting ETF Information: The ETF is highly specialized by type of company, sector, region or country, or index. There are hundreds of ETFs to choose from. Two valuable sites are Morningstar at http://www.morning star.com/Cover/ETF.html?pgid = hec1tabetf, and Yahoo! Finance at http://finance.yahoo.com/etf.

Another Look at Options

Direct ownership of stocks or utilizing mutual funds or ETFs are the most popular and safest methods of investing for most people. Interest in the stock market invariably leads new investors to these avenues. However, it is also useful, especially for those who have gained some seasoning in the market, to continue thinking about options as tools for managing a portfolio: reducing risk by protecting paper profits (buying puts), taking advantage of price dips (buying calls), or creating additional income with no added market risk (writing covered calls).

Additional uses of options appeal to many investors. If you want to use a small portion of your available capital to speculate, especially if you see an opportunity developing, options are a great alternative to buying additional stock. Most people are frustrated, because with limited capital resources they cannot take advantage of all the bargain prices they see in volatile markets. Options are the perfect solution. For relatively small amounts of cash (thus, lower market risks), you can control 100 shares of stock for each option purchased for a fraction of the cost of buying shares. Even if you want to buy an odd lot, options are cheaper. Today, the cost of buying five or 10 shares of stock is not much greater than the cost of trading in round lots of 100 shares. Consider this example: Let's say a stock was selling at $58–$60 per share and the market as a whole falls. The stock drops to $50 and you think the price is going to rebound very quickly. But with only about $500 available, you can only buy 10 shares, meaning you cannot take full advantage of the price decline. However, you could buy a call option for about $500 that controls 100 shares of stock, potentially resulting in 10 times more profit over buying 10 shares.

Pure speculation is not a wise move for most investors, at least not with large portions of a limited capital resource. But there are times when prices move quickly and, as is usually the case, to an exaggerated level. Markets tend to overreact. So if a triple-digit price decline drags down a stock that is otherwise reasonably priced, it is probable that the price will rebound. In these circumstances you can use options to create additional profits from short-term speculation.

One technique that was popular in the past was day trading, a technique of moving in and out of positions within a single day. The day trader epitomized leverage by closing out all positions before the end of trading. A brokerage's margin requirements are based on end-of-day positions, so it was possible to execute a high volume of trades without getting any margin calls. This high-risk strategy created a lot of wealth in the past during times when the markets were rising, but also led to many large losses. When day traders were not able to close their positions at a profit, brokerages often were left with huge losses.

To offset this situation, the SEC enacted the *pattern day trader* rule in 2001. Under this rule, any time a trader moves in and out of the same position four or more times over five consecutive trading days they must leave at least $25,000 on deposit in their trading accounts in cash and equities. Also, if the number of round-trip (buy and sell) day trades exceed 6 percent of the total trades in an account, that person is also a pattern day trader. This also triggers the requirement to have at least $25,000.

A variation of day trading is *swing trading*. This is a pattern of moving in and out of positions in a three- to five-day period. It is a perfect solution to avoid the pattern day trader rule, and it is also a good way to make profits from extremely short-term price swings. The swing trader recognizes that the market is ruled by emotions, specifically greed and fear. As a consequence of these emotions, price movements tend to be overreactions causing very short-term "swing" opportunities. Prices are likely to move too far based on any current news. Swing traders move into long positions at the bottom of short-term swings and sell at the top. On the short side, they may sell short at the top in anticipation of the price retreating and close at the bottom. However, by using options, short selling can be avoided. At the top, swing traders can buy puts instead of selling stock.

Using options enables swing traders to restrict themselves to long positions only, which is much less risky than short selling. Buying either calls (at a price bottom) or puts (at a price top) limits exposure and potential loss. It also provides effective leverage. Because a single option controls 100 shares of stock, swing traders can expand their potential profits to more actual shares of stock in a short-term price movement, as well as to more companies. Because options cost much less than stock they are more flexible.

Swing traders look for specific patterns to time their trades. When a stock's price follows a downtrend for three or more days, swing traders look for a purchase setup. A downtrend is defined as a series of trading days where the daily closing price is lower, and where the trading range combines a series of progressively lower low prices and lower high prices. On the other side, swing traders look for a price reversal after an uptrend. This is three or more days of progressively higher closing prices, in which the daily trading range is a combination of progressively higher high and higher low prices.

The setup may involve one or more of the following patterns as well. First is a narrow-range day, in which the distance between low and high price is extremely small. Second is a reversal day, in which the established trend turns in the opposite direction. Third is a day with exceptionally high volume, especially if the trading range is also narrow. The existence of any two of these set-up signals is strong; if all three are present (narrow-range day, reversal day, and high volume), it is practically certain that the trend is over and prices will begin moving in the opposite direction.

Swing trading is an interesting price-based technique, and if you are able to keep an eye on price movement from day to day, it is an action-packed and exciting method for speculating in the market. Using options also makes swing trading far easier for most people, compared to transacting in long or short positions using shares of stock.

Whether you use options as pure speculation within your portfolio, or in a more conservative vein (covered call writing, for example), option trading is complex and may come with many dangers. The range of trading strategies covers the entire spectrum from high risk to very conservative, so it is crucial to study and understand the market before embarking on any one strategy. Simply knowing the actual risk is an important step in trading options and, in fact, for any other type of strategy.

You can learn a lot about options by studying the information on the option industry's Options Clearing Corporation (OCC) Web site, which can be accessed at *www.optionsclearing.com*. This site offers a free copy of the prospectus for the options industry, "Characteristics and Risks of Standardized Options," as well as many other free products and services including access to education on options. You may also check the Chicago Board Options Exchange (CBOE) at *www.cboe.com*. The CBOE provides educational courses as well as free option quotes, data and statistics, detailed explanations of various strategies, an online options bookstore, and their own training and educational courses. Both the OCC and CBOE Web sites are valuable resources to expand your knowledge of the options market.

The next chapter moves the discussion of alternative investing strategies to a related and important topic, market timing. By looking for methods to analyze current market conditions, you can improve the timing of buy or sell decisions and thus improve overall performance and profitability in your portfolio.

MARKET TIMING

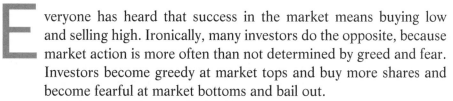veryone has heard that success in the market means buying low and selling high. Ironically, many investors do the opposite, because market action is more often than not determined by greed and fear. Investors become greedy at market tops and buy more shares and become fearful at market bottoms and bail out.

After considering the building blocks presented in preceding chapters, an astute investor analyzes conditions for a specific stock to determine if or when to take action in the market. Timing should be based on an analysis of earnings and profits; the requirements for diversification as qualified by application of Charles Dow's ideas (which are, essentially, programmed trend analysis models); tests such as volatility (price as well as fundamental); and a careful study of the P/E ratio trend.

■ Buy Low, Sell High

The best-known stock market maxim, "buy low, sell high" sounds obvious and trite. But actually, it is quite profound when you realize that many investors do just the opposite. The market is governed by two emotions: greed (on the upside) and fear (on the downside). The way that many investors and traders make decisions is also emotional and lacks the calm, analytical approach that invariably leads to better timing of decisions. In fact, the *contrarian* (an investor who goes against the majority) takes advantage of the usual market tendency, buying when everyone else is selling and selling when everyone else is buying. Put the contrarian model in a different light and consider the emotional aspects. While the crowd emotionally reacts and overreacts to changes in price, the contrarian takes a step back, analyzes what is going on, and times decisions without emotion.

The classic investor mentality is reactive but blind. When prices are rising the typical investor wants to jump in, buying shares in accelerating stocks to get in on the action. This greed tends to accelerate as stock prices reach a peak, meaning that more and more investors and traders buy at or near the top. Why do stocks stop rising and turn around? That is the question. The reason is that at some point, the price inertia runs its course and demand saturates. Buying demand no longer keeps up, simply due to the fact that all of the buyers have taken positions. At this point the wise trader knows it is time to take profits, and selling pressure replaces buying pressure. Aggravating this situation, short sellers also recognize that the top is at hand and they begin to sell the stock, which further accelerates the selling action. Those traders who acted out of greed and entered long positions near the top invariably end up losing, because prices begin to fall. They ignored the advice to "buy low" and instead decided to "buy high." This sequence repeats itself over and over.

The same thing happens at the bottom. When investors and traders take up long positions in stock, they almost always assume (and believe) that their entry price is zero and that the stock must rise from that point onward. This ignores the reality that prices go up *and* down. When prices fall significantly the greed response is replaced, often very quickly, by the fear response. As prices fall, sellers fuel the drop but at some point, all long position sellers have executed trades. At the very bottom, an accelerated level of selling causes a lot of activity. At this point, investors on the sidelines recognize a bargain price and a buying opportunity and they begin to buy. Buying demand replaces the selling activity, and is made even more extreme as short sellers cover their positions with more buy orders. Those investors who operate out of fear sell their stock at the worst possible time. Instead of following the advice to "sell high," they do the opposite; they "sell low."

The net outcome of this greed-and-fear mode is that many traders end up with a "buy high, sell low" approach, the opposite of what they should be doing. But taking the advice to "buy low, sell high" is not easy. It is compelling to listen to the majority and fall into the greed trap as prices rise or into the fear trap as prices fall. Taking a calmer, more rational approach makes perfect sense but it demands discipline.

It is that one attribute—discipline—that defines successful investors and traders. The timing of decisions can be made in several ways:

1. *Emotional and reactive.* The most common form of timing is a train wreck in your portfolio. It causes great harm to your portfolio's net worth to act emotionally as both greed and fear lead to poor decisions. If you react to what everyone else is doing, you will be wrong most of the time. This is why shooting from the hip in the market, which may occasionally result in fast and easy profits, is a losing battle. Eventually, the poorly timed decisions will outpace the lucky, well-timed decisions.

2. *Short term and exploitive.* An equally damaging policy is to think short term and violate your own investing goals. For example, if you sell stock any time a small profit appears in the price, you will miss opportunities. If you picked a good company for all of the fundamentally right reasons, taking profits does not make sense. Short-term prices swing up and down and you might be able to get back into the stock at a lower price. But if the price continues moving upward, you lose that opportunity forever. Even more of a problem is that when you sell only those stocks that become slightly profitable, you end up with a portfolio of underperforming stocks. By attrition, you end up selling the winners and holding the losers. It is also short-term thinking to panic and sell stock if its market

value falls a few points. Remember, if you picked a company for the right reasons, a short-term price decline is not permanent.

3. *Contrarian and analytical.* The sensible timing approach is to act as a contrarian and rely on sound analysis. Contrarian investing is most commonly thought of as simply doing the opposite of the majority, but that is only part of the bigger picture. A contrarian also applies discipline to resist the all-too-easy emotions that rule market thinking. Everyone feels the emotions. When the market falls in triple digits in a matter of hours, you wonder whether you have picked the wrong stocks. When the market rises in triple digits, you wish you had bought more. These greed and fear reactions are human. But acting on these emotions is a mistake and leads to poor timing.

Market Emotions and Their Effect

It is worth exploring the nature of greed and fear a little bit further to better understand how to develop a smart timing policy. If you really want to "buy low, sell high," you need to recognize when your instincts are right *and* when they are wrong.

Instincts are actually informed opinions. Your timing about when to buy or sell shares might be based on your instincts, and as long as your fundamental and technical analysis support that opinion you will do well to follow them. Question why you are thinking of buying or selling. Do you have a sound reason? For example, if a company's latest earnings are higher than everyone thought and the fundamentals (such as debt ratio, net income, and dividends) are strong, those are all good signs. But what if the stock's price has fallen along with the rest of the market? If the price today is lower than you believe the stock is worth, then it is a bargain. If your instincts—accompanied by the signs you find in your analysis—tell you to buy, then you should buy. But if your instincts are emotional and without any good reason, then buying is probably a mistake.

The same rationale applies to selling. Before selling, consider the nature of fear as part of your analysis. For example, if you bought shares of stock because all of the fundamentals were what you expected from a company, then you probably made a good decision. If dividend yield is high and P/E is low, while revenues and profits grow each year and the company is exceptionally well managed, all of the signs support your decision to buy and hold that stock. But what if the price falls? In fact, if your original reasons for buying continue to apply, you should *not* sell out of fear. As long as the numbers still look right, hang tough and do nothing, or buy more shares at the current bargain price.

The rational, analytical approach also has limits, of course. People tend to rationalize, even when their decisions turn out to be poor ones. And everyone makes timing mistakes, even with the most thorough analysis. For example, what if you bought shares in a company based on good fundamentals, but the picture has recently changed?

For example, in mid-2007, a lot of financial stocks looked good even as the credit crunch and housing subprime problems were accelerating. Shares of Citigroup, Bank of America, and Washington Mutual were considered by most analysts to be sound investments. The dividend yields were exceptional, profits high, and prospects positive. But by autumn, those same companies had been downgraded, stock prices fell to as much as one-half their summer levels, and the likelihood of recovery seemed remote at best. Anyone who bought shares in these companies in summer 2007 had made a mistake.

Does this mean those people should have sold their shares at one-half the purchase value? Even though buying these companies at their market value in the summer turned out to be poor timing, the decision to sell should be based on fundamentals and not on the basis of fear. Most financial companies faced the prospect of substantial losses based on subprime problems, but in the long term were they "bad" investments? No one can read the future, but you can make decisions based on strong fundamentals and the prospects of cyclical turnarounds.

The financial stocks, like all sectors, go through cyclical changes and history shows that even with bad timing and poor decisions, it is not always wise to "cut your losses." In some cases, you simply have to hold on and ride through the downturns and wait until the sector begins to move in a positive direction. The bottom line is this: If you buy stock for the right reasons, a downturn is always a temporary problem and eventually the stock price will rebound. You only lose permanently when you buy inflated-value stocks at exceptionally high prices, and the decline in value is a return to a more realistic level.

This distinction is a critical one. There is a tendency in the market to believe that all price movement is the same, and that it always occurs for the same reasons. But in fact, there are many different reasons for stock prices to change. An overpriced stock (recognized by extremely high P/E and a rapid, irrational increase in price levels, for example) is likely to fall rapidly when market-wide prices decline. A well-priced stock may also follow broader trends in price, and a decline to bargain price levels is typically followed by a return to a reasonable price.

Relying on the Fundamentals: Growth Versus Value

Just as price movement cannot be assumed to occur for the same reasons in all cases, not every stock reacts to market conditions in the same manner. Volatility is often determined by sector, overall market conditions, the way a company is managed, its competitive position, or the long-term cyclical conditions for a specific sector.

Reliance on fundamentals is the best way to avoid big mistakes. This reality has been proven over and over. If you look back at history, you quickly realize that exceptionally strong companies (in terms of fundamentals) perform well in all kinds of markets and any decline in price tends to be temporary. By the same argument, companies with weak fundamentals may rise in some markets, but they tend to perform poorly over the long term. Strong fundamentals in the volatile year 2007 created a lot of price chaos. Even so, strong value companies like Altria, Coca-Cola, Exxon-Mobil, McDonald's, and Merck had strong price rises in 2007. Even while the DJIA fell from 14,000 to the high 12,000s level, the fundamentally strong companies simply continued to rise in price throughout the year. It was as though these stocks were immune to the chaotic price swings that affected the brokerages, banks, and big mortgage lenders. What did these companies have in common?

It is really quite simple. In fact, it is so simple that even before the volatility of 2007, a short list of value stocks would have led to a strong, profitable portfolio. The value investing approach is always wise, and timing of purchases of these stocks should be based on fundamental strength in the company versus technical volatility in the market as a whole. In other words, the more you see triple-digit movement in the indices, the more you should retreat to the safer, stronger companies. Their common attributes include exceptional management, strong profitability, dominance in their sectors, and low core earnings adjustments. The core earnings observation is based on a reality about the way the fundamentals work. You will find that the lower the annual core earnings adjustments, the more stable the stock price tends to be. This is not a blanket truth, but the tendency does hold. In fact, companies with little or no core earnings adjustments also tend to report gradually rising stock price values over time. They are immune to short-term volatility in the sense that their value simply continues to grow each year.

In addition to the basic fundamental tests, you will find that these value companies tend to report consistent or increasing dividends each year, and maintain low debt ratios and low P/E ratios in all kinds of market conditions. A value approach to investing may be accurately described as finding well-managed companies that are immune to the short-term chaos of markets, as seen in index point changes.

Many analysts make a distinction between value and growth, and you may often hear the odd description of market activity as a "retreat to value." This description is odd because value should be in season in all conditions. But some investors find value companies boring and too slow moving compared to the faster action in "growth" stocks. The definition of growth is elusive, however. The most popular definition is that a "growth" stock is one for a company whose earnings are outpacing the average of its industry. They tend to pay little or no dividends, based on the argument that profits are better used to fund future growth. Many investors are enamored with stocks like Google, whose market value has been impressive.

But when you look at Google's fundamentals, questions have to be raised concerning market risk and safety.

Some of the fundamentals are very positive. Debt ratio is close to zero and core earnings adjustments are quite small. However, some other indicators are troubling. For example, the market price of Google as of early December 2007 was $684 per share (with a 52-week range of $437–$747), but tangible book value per share was only $49 as of the latest fiscal year end. No dividends were paid and the most disturbing ratio was the P/E, at 53.

Even with many strong fundamentals, the zero dividend and exceptionally high P/E make Google a classic growth stock. But with such a high P/E and volatile price movement, the stock also contains exceptional market risk. The potential for strong growth is always accompanied by equally strong market risk, and that is the point. So a "retreat to value," which often is expressed as a negative sign in the market, is actually quite prudent. Price action in the financial markets in 2007 (previously considered to be solid stocks without exception) demonstrates that the retreat often represents simple, prudent investing and smart timing.

Studying Stocks in Terms of Value and Growth

The selection criteria for stocks can and should include a study of both fundamental and technical indicators. Limiting selection to companies with exceptionally strong fundamentals is an important starting point, because these tend to report lower price volatility, faster recovery from price declines, and long-term value *and* growth. The alternative of picking stocks solely for the purpose of growth, without consideration of fundamental strength or sector position, is highly speculative.

Even so, growth can and does occur among value stocks, as the volatile history of the 2007 stock market demonstrated. Criteria for selection may include many important attributes combining both fundamental and technical indicators. A limited number of important indicators should provide enough information to determine which stocks offer the most suitable and promising market performance with minimal risk. These criteria may include:

- Steadily growing revenues *and* net profit with low fundamental volatility
- Little or no core earnings adjustments
- Annual growth in dividends for at least 10 years
- P/E ratio between limited ranges, such as 10 to 25
- Steady or declining debt ratio, preferably on the low side
- Exceptional management reputation over many years
- Leading competitive position within a sector
- Moderate to low trading range over the past year
- Ten-year trend of rising stock prices, not falling prices

Certainly, additional criteria can be included. However, using all of these indicators helps narrow down a list to a few exceptionally strong investment candidates. Are they, by definition, *value* stocks? They probably are, but this definition must also include price considerations. The ideal growth stock also has to be priced at a bargain, and this is where market timing is so important. You can easily buy a stock at an inflated price, even if it is a value stock. This only means that it will take longer to realize a profit. But even the best stocks are likely to follow market trends. In volatile markets characterized by many triple-digit moves, you will see stock values decline by 4 or 5 percent in a single day, and sometimes by more. Assuming all of the other selection criteria are in place, it makes sense to buy shares of exceptional value companies at times when prices have fallen. This pattern represents a dip in the price wave and not an emerging negative trend. When a company reports strong fundamentals over a decade and the price action follows suit, it *is* a value company.

Some will point to the negative experience with companies like Enron, claiming that it is possible for unethical management to "cook the books" and report positive fundamentals even when the whole thing is falling apart. This is true, but only over a period of two or three years. Cooking the books eventually gets found out, and it is impossible for any company to fool investors for a complete decade. So if you look only at the current indicators and do not include a full 10-year study of the important trends, then it is possible to be deceived. Cases like Enron make this point quite well. Enron's price and reporting history was extremely short term. Management fooled most people, including the prestigious Dow Jones Company, which had added Enron to its utility averages in 1997, before its book-cooking ways were revealed. Four years later, in 2001, Enron was removed from the index. The whole Enron mess took place over only a few short years; in fact, the bigger the scale of deception, the more difficult it is to continue it for any length of time.

It is certain that future financial scandals will erupt, even among companies with long-standing financial reports. But it is easy to spot emerging or questionable trends. Whenever the financial picture looks unusually good after a period of relatively low volatility, question it. When a company reports a single year with a spike in earnings, you should be dubious. Well-managed companies tend to report fairly consistent outcomes unless extraordinary events (like mergers and acquisitions, class action lawsuits, or labor strikes) occur. These aberrations are easily explained. It is the unexplained and odd variation away from a trend that should raise suspicion.

It is ironic that in the greed- and fear-dominated market some investors do not raise questions even when they should. Many thousands of people put too much money into Enron stock and did not ask questions, simply accepting the huge paper profits derived from growing stock prices. It would have been wise to ask questions, but in a market where profits continue occurring month after month, the common tendency is to not question the trend and just assume—unrealistically—that it will continue forever. The sad outcome is that eventually those cooked books catch up and the whole price structure evaporates, usually overnight. You would think that investors would learn from the Enron experience, especially those who lost their life savings, but unfortunately, these self-delusional tendencies are repeated time and again.

To avoid making these kinds of mistakes, avoid the temptation to let your timing and stock selection be based on greed and fear. Thorough, careful analysis is much less interesting—and some would even call it boring—but ultimately, you will end up with less risk and more profits than those willing to speculate in pursuit of fast and easy profits. They often discover, too late, that fast and easy losses are more likely.

▪ The Short-Term Temptation

Besides the advice to "buy low, sell high," another bit of market wisdom informs you that "the market rewards patience." No matter how much experience you accumulate as an investor, you can never remind yourself too often about how true this is.

The impatience of many investors leads to ill timing and even to the selection of the wrong stocks. Short-term thinking comes with many self-destructive attributes, including:

1. *The tendency to sell too quickly.* When investors think in terms of today, this week, and this month they lose sight of the long term. Even if their stated investment goals include a "buy and hold" strategy involving value stocks, once prices rise slightly the tendency is to take profits. This is self-destructive. It turns investors with conservative risk profiles into speculators with high-risk profiles; in other words, short-term thinking can and does destroy an investor's objectives. Stating the objective is only the first step; following your own rules demands consistency and discipline, and this is where the task is much more difficult.

2. *Moving in and out of stocks when price action is not fast enough.* Another attribute of short-term thinking is seen in the addiction to action. Traders like to be players and to move in and out of positions and watch their values change by the hour, or even by the minute. It is very exciting to double your money in a single, five-minute trade. Even though this does happen, it is as easy to lose half of your money just as quickly. The addiction to the action can be self-defeating.

3. *Failure to recognize or appreciate long-term value.* Short-term traders have no interest in holding onto stocks for many years, or even for a few months. Their impatience tells them that if they don't make a double-digit return in a matter of weeks, their money is sitting idle. But in many sound investments, it is necessary to wait out the market. In conditions of great volatility, growth stocks may gain or lose double-digit percentages of value, compared to value stocks that tend to rise slowly and steadily over time. Even in a down market, well-selected stocks outperform the averages simply by holding their value. As long as stocks inch upward, even in a sideways market you may beat the average by reinvesting dividends and waiting for the benefits over time.

The point to remember is this: Market timing requires intelligent analysis to be effective. Anyone who relies on unsupported instinct and who acts based on greed and fear is going to buy high and sell low. This is self-defeating. When you pick solid, well-managed, competitive, strong companies, the day-to-day price movement does not matter; you are more interested in the long term.

In volatile markets, you serve your interest well by holding onto well-picked value stocks and using options to take profits or to buy at advantageously low price levels. By leaving most of your capital invested in exceptionally good companies, you ultimately prove that "timing" is often a matter of waiting over a period of months or years. As long as your overall profits benefit from this strategy, any short-term opportunities you might lose will be found in a sea of potential losses of equal potential.

The next chapter concludes the discussion of stock investing by summarizing the major points that determine the health and safety of your portfolio. A wise investor knows that continually evaluating, thinking into the future, and pondering risk are the keys to building wealth and to protecting yourself. Remember, all losses are unexpected, whereas consistent profits are planned. As the next chapter explains, setting your risk profile and investment policy define the kind of investments you should make.

28.92   21.96 5   29.47
21.95   29.47 272   488.06
29.46   488.19 3
88.07   117.02 9   117.02
7.00   20.84
20.84 370

C H A P T E R   1 2

APPLYING YOUR COMPREHENSIVE PROGRAM

You will benefit by applying all of the information presented in this book, which is designed to help you make *informed* market decisions. All of the factors and tools for analysis, tempered by an awareness of how they commonly are misapplied, show the investor how to make *valid* comparisons in order to arrive at sensible decisions.

A common problem in the market is to use the wrong information, or to apply the right information in the wrong way. For example, an investor might buy a stock because it has a high P/E ratio and because the DJIA is on the rise. Neither of these factors actually reveal whether the company represents a timely investment, and the decision does not address the issues that should be at the heart of the decision.

The recent past is quite revealing. Thousands of investors bought shares of Amazon.com over many years and the values kept rising. However, the company only recently began earning a profit.

So what was the basis for the decision? Shake-out in dot.com companies overall have made the following point: The majority of investment decisions are made with a lack of information after looking at the wrong indicators, or are based on the desire to make quick and easy profits without foundation in the company itself.

This chapter demonstrates how the short list of ideas introduced in the preceding chapters are used together to develop a powerful, well-based program that will improve profits and protect investors against common mistakes.

Seven Market Myths

The stock market is a place where magical thinking rules, where superstition and easily disproved beliefs rule, and where luck is considered as valid a guiding force as earnings per share (EPS); perhaps luck is even the stronger force.

The market feeds itself on rumor, myth, gossip, and odd beliefs about money itself. For example, many people believe that there is a finite amount of *value* in the world. If this is true, anyone who makes money from buying a stock is taking that money away from someone else. This is clearly untrue. In a free market economy, wealth is created out of profits. As a corporation earns profits, it pays taxes that fund governments on federal and state levels; it creates jobs and ensures a healthy economy for families, leading to wealth accumulation through savings, home ownership, and investment; and it fuels innovation and invention to keep the economy competitive on a global level.

The profit motive is a positive force. Every invention has been driven by a profit motive and successful invention has been rewarded well in the market. Computers, the Internet, digital cameras, cell phones, ever-smaller communication devices, safer consumer products, and fuel-efficient appliances and automobiles—the list of improvements in technology is endless. Quality of life and longevity itself continue to improve as the profit motive drives the economy forward. The average life expectancy in the United States has nearly doubled in the past 150 years. The increase in life expectancy reflects improved healthcare, diet, and environmental conditions:

Life Expectancy in the United States:[1]

	Caucasian Only		Non-Caucasian Only	
Year	Men	Women	Men	Women
1850	38	41	Not Available	
1900	48	51	33	35
1950	66	72	59	63
2000	75	80	68	75

This does not mean that profits in the stock market is solely responsible for the higher life expectancy in the United States today. However, the profit motive has fueled innovation and it is the intrinsic uniting feature in the free market economy. In fact, the twentieth-century experiment with Communism in many parts of the world makes the same point in the negative. Life expectancy in the previous USSR and more recently, in Russia, has been consistently lower than in the United States. There may be many reasons, including well-known chronic heart disease and cancer rates, but this also raises the question about better health in free market economies versus poorer health in state-controlled economies.

As an investor, dealing with the myths about how markets work is a wise step in mastering stock market theories and practice. In a free economy, the profit motive is a driving force that increases tax revenues and creates jobs and ultimately leads to better health and safe environments. As a stockholder, you participate in this vibrant economic growth. As the market itself grows into a global force for change, the entire world economy is likely to benefit from the historical forward-moving themes so consistently seen in the United States.

However, myths continue to dominate the market. Part of the stock market culture is based on a few common threads. Seven of the most persistent market myths are:

1. *The only way to invest is to buy and hold for the long term.* The well-known "value investor" is a very conservative individual

who believes that you cannot make money by moving in and out of positions. The idea is to find a good company, buy its stock, and then literally forget about it for many years, or even for decades. The extreme devotee of value investing believes that you should buy and hold for decades rather than for years, but this is questionable as a hard-and-fast policy in a quickly changing world. For example, 10 or 20 years ago, most people would have agreed that companies like Eastman Kodak, General Motors, and Polariod were premium value companies that conservative investors should hold for the long term. But even over a 10-year period, the fortunes of these companies declined. Changing technology and new forms of competition have made many past beliefs about these companies obsolete today. The "right" holding period of a company must be based on a continual review of the overall market and of each market sector. This does not mean you need to spend many hours per day studying the market, but you need to be aware of a reality: Today's "excellent stock" is likely to go through changes in the future, and some of those changes will create obsolescence of product or of management beliefs.

2. *You should have done something different in the past.* Investors have been known to beat themselves up over missed opportunities or poorly timed decisions. Regret is popular but nonproductive. It tends to destroy your self-confidence and leads you to question your own good ideas. Overthinking past mistakes is destructive and makes too many people excessively risk-adverse, so that (ironically) they miss future opportunities as a result. A more sensible approach is to learn from mistakes and then move beyond them. If the strategies you employ and the analysis you apply make sense in most situations, don't waver. You are going to make mistakes and suffer losses; everyone who invests money in stocks will experience downward price movement at some time. But that does not mean your strategies are flawed. Truly successful investors experience a reduced rate of losses because their analytical approach is intelligent. Don't allow yourself to suffer from the myth that "good" investors do not make mistakes. The truth is that good investors are those who learn from their mistakes.

3. *Tips point the way to exceptional value.* The insidious belief in the reliable rumor has caused more mischief in the market's history than any other force. It is the basis of greed and fear and it overrules all rational, analytical thought. Many investors are fast to react to a well-placed tip, even without first asking whether it is true. There is an ever-present sense that decisions must be made *right now* or the chance will be lost forever. For example, if the tip is that a stock's value is going to rise in the next few days, the tendency is to buy without applying sensible tests. If the rumors say that a stock is about to lose value, the tendency is to sell or to get out before those losses occur.

It is a smart approach to try and ignore *all* rumors. Even going onto investment chat lines can be a problem, because you have no way of knowing who the people are that are making claims. The truth is, those who really know what is going on in a company are not going onto chat lines to share information with the world. In fact, there really are no good tips. Even if there were good ways to get the inside scoop, it is against the law to act on that information. People go to prison for making trades based on information not known to the general public. A favorite online pastime is the *pump and dump*. Someone owns shares in a company and they chat up the stock on chat lines by spreading rumors about takeover announcements about to be made, new products, and as yet unannounced good news. The purpose is to drive up the price of the stock, with the idea of selling it when the price goes up. The pump and dump is illegal, but this practice continues to occur.

4. *Big institutions have special knowledge individuals do not have.* Mutual funds, insurance companies, pension plan administrators—in other words, "professional" managers—are believed to have exceptional skills in picking stocks and in timing their market decisions. But history contradicts this belief. Only about 10 percent of all mutual funds outperform the S&P 500, for example. The overall record of mutual fund performance is quite dismal, and the only way to "beat the averages" is to reinvest earnings. The long-term effect of compounding is quite amazing, even at a dismal rate of return. For example, what does it mean when you read that "if

you had invested $10,000 only 20 years ago in this fund, your account would be worth $26,500 today"? In fact, it means the average return was only 5 percent per year, and that all earnings were reinvested. But there are flaws in this assumption. First, no allowance is included for taxes so the after-tax compounded rate would be much lower. Second, the mutual fund picks its date for making this claim. If you put a lump sum of money into a fund when prices were high and they later fell, you would not enjoy the average return. This illustration also fails to discount the overall return for the numerous fees charged by the fund.

Realistically, institutional performance in the market has been very poor, proving that even the most skilled professional managers really do not have an inside track on picking stocks. Furthermore, the incentives for timing are often not in the best interests of stockholders. Fund management has been known to time buy and sell decisions to reflect the best possible quarter-end report of their performance. It is possible a fund will sell a company's stock to bolster its overall return, even if the indications are that the stock should be kept in the portfolio longer. You can reinvest dividends in individual stocks, or make other market decisions on your own; compared to many of the mega-funds with billions of dollars under management, individuals have much greater flexibility and can buy or sell within moments. A big fund with broadly diversified holdings cannot make portfolio-wide decisions quickly, because their holdings in individual stocks may be too large. In addition, because a fund has to limit its percentage of ownership in any one company, it may be necessary to diversify so broadly that overall returns will suffer. Mutual fund investing can be quite profitable, but a realistic conclusion has to be that "exceptional management knowledge" should not be a primary reason to choose them.

5. *Diversification is boring; you should go for profits instead.* The speculative approach—seeking fast profits by placing money in single stocks—is appealing. The "greed factor" dominates speculative thinking and some speculators may experience one dazzling success after another, for a while. But greed also mandates that profits be churned back into positions for even higher profits. It

takes only one badly timed decision to wipe out all of the profits accumulated over many months. Sadly, many speculators act solely on the basis of greed and they do not understand risk. Diversification may be boring, but so is quietly making consistent, small profits. An effectively diversified portfolio will weather all kinds of markets. In exceptionally strong bull markets diversified investors will not make the same double-digit profits that speculators will make, but in flat or falling markets they will do much better.

6. *You should find a bargain stock and buy as much as you can today.* A popular approach in the past has been to move 100-share or higher increments into stock positions. One reason was that round-lot trading was more affordable than odd-lot trading. But today, with low-cost online brokerage services, you can buy any number of shares, even single shares, and not pay much more than you pay for 100-share trades. But this is a myth for another reason: It often makes more sense to buy smaller increments of a stock, wait for short-term declines in price, and then buy more at relatively bargain-level prices. All stocks move around short term, rising and falling from day to day even when the longer-term trend is upward. You can easily identify peaks and valleys and time incremental purchases. This is more prudent than buying an entire position in a single trade.

7. *The entry price is "zero" and the stock has to rise from there.* This myth has been referred to a few times in past chapters, but is worth emphasizing again. Many people wrongly believe that the price at which shares are bought is the starting point; they expect the price to go up from there. As a consequence, they are taken by surprise when the price falls. In fact, any price is simply the latest reflection of a never-ending struggle between buyers and sellers. Prices rise and fall over time and trends get established. It is a big error to fall into the belief that a particular price is "zero."

In seeking value for your dollar, you may begin with a fundamental analysis of the stock to determine what you would consider "fair market value" for the stock, including growth potential (especially as reflected in the P/E ratio level, for example, in which you limit the selection criteria to a specific range). Once you decide on what you believe is a fair price per share, you seek opportunities in the price movement. For example, a company may have a record-setting year of higher revenues and profits and all indicators are strong. But if the EPS were two or three cents lower than estimates published by Wall Street analysts, the stock price might fall on the day earnings are published. In some cases, the price may fall several points. It is important to realize that such a price decline is an extreme overreaction to news. This means that within the coming trading days, the price is very likely to return to a more rational level. If the cause of the decline were due to excessive selling and the recognition of the price as a bargain level brings in buyers, it will drive the price back up. This is typical of how prices move short term and why they change at all. But no price is "zero" for the buyer; it is an ongoing struggle between buyers and sellers. Recognizing this gives you an advantage in the market, because you will be able to sit on the sidelines and recognize when the price dips below the rational trading range and then make your move.

Determining the Validity of Information and Applying It Correctly: The Right Assumptions

Stockholders are often information junkies who, in addition to operating on many myth-based assumptions, often do not know what to believe or how much weight to give to information. The distinction between reliable action-generating news and everything else can be an impediment to making sound investment decisions.

There is so much information available that it is difficult to sort through it. This is why the suggestion makes sense to limit your analysis to a short list of a few fundamental and technical indicators. By applying these consistently, you keep the list of stocks short and consider only the highest-caliber listed companies.

Even a promising bit of news or financial report can be misleading. You only need to go back to 2000 and 2001 and read the glowing reports about Enron—as a company and as a stock—to realize that you do not always get the truth. If you read annual reports, you also get a slanted view of matters. Companies whose financial strength has declined over the past decade continue to make bold claims in their annual reports about how much everything is about to improve. Read the annual reports of Eastman Kodak (whose stock values have plunged as its primary product, film, has become increasingly obsolete), and you will discover just how severe the problem is with what companies tell their investors.

Eastman Kodak's 2006 annual report made bold claims. This company, whose stock price during 2006 ranged between $19 and $31 per share versus 1997 levels between $53 and $95, claims to be in the middle of an impressive turnaround; this remains to be seen. Kodak's problems are profound. For example, its debt ratio rose over 10 years from 15.6 percent up to 66.2 percent by 2006, primarily due to its inability to recognize the importance of emerging digital camera technology. With its major product old-style film, for many years Kodak continued to believe it would remain a dominant force in that market, failing to see that the market itself was rapidly disappearing. In the 2006 annual report, Kodak's chairman wrote that "We have met unprecedented challenges in the company's history and we are becoming a stronger company in the process. Moreover, we're within sight of completing what will be one of the most remarkable turnarounds in corporate history."[2]

If you knew nothing about the history of Eastman Kodak and the only information you had available was its annual report, what would you think? It is clearly foolish to buy stock in a company based on the hype written in the annual report, which is part regulatory compliance and part public relations. It would make more sense to apply a short list of sensible fundamental and technical tests. If you were to use the tests recommended in Chapter 5, companies like Eastman Kodak would not qualify as a viable investment. Those 10 key fundamental and technical indicators are:

1. P/E ratio
2. Trading range
3. Trading volatility
4. Current ratio *and* debt ratio
5. Current yield

6. Dividend growth

7. Revenue and net profits

8. Fundamental volatility

9. Net income *and* core net income

10. Competitive status, management, and credit rating

It is always prudent in studying indicators to not only check the current status, but to look for the trend over a 10-year period. This reveals the direction of improvement or deterioration. Clearly, a 10-year study of these indicators for extremes (such as Wal-Mart versus General Motors, or Altria versus Eastman Kodak) make the following point: Financial strength and performance is important, but the 10-year trend reveals the whole story. If a company's numbers are sliding for 10 years, why should you believe they will turn around? They might, but there comes a point where a company's condition has deteriorated so far that recovery becomes unlikely. With General Motor's debt ratio above 100 percent it means the equity value of the company is negative. How does a company recover from that and how long will it take?

It is true that a weakened company may be priced at bargain levels. But a very weak company, especially one with extraordinary debt levels, has burdened itself with problems that will not turn around in a few months or even a few years. The assumptions you use should make sense, and when you see falling profits, falling stock prices, and rising long-term debt, those companies are clearly not worthwhile long-term value investments.

■ The Market of the Future: A Triple-Digit Norm?

Moving beyond the analysis using a short list of indicators, you also need to consider what the stock market is going to look like in the future. The market is dynamic and reflects a constantly changing global market and economy. Many factors have changed the market itself as well as its accessibility. Major changes over the past two decades include:

1. *Expansion of world markets.* With the end of the Communist regime that lasted about 70 years, barriers to international trade came down, most notably in Europe. This alone vastly expanded trade potential and increased interaction in worldwide markets. The involvement of China, the last remaining major Communist state in the world, in international trade has only accelerated the rate of expansion.

2. *Internet access and improved information and communications.* Before the Internet, transactions as simple as placement of a trade on the market was cumbersome and expensive. An individual investor had to telephone a stockbroker, ask for quotes, and make a trade decision. The stockbroker had to either telephone a trader on the floor of the exchange or communicate via a very slow and limited quotations and order-placement system, which was usually located in a "wire house," a specialized area of the brokerage firm. This was time-consuming for everyone involved and when the order volume was heavy, there were numerous places along the way that prevented fast order placement. These included the stockbroker's telephone and all subsequent steps.

Today, every investor can easily place his or her own trades from a home computer with Internet access, or at a system in the workplace. It is virtually immediate, cheap, and fast. The requirement for old-style trading became obsolete in less than two decades.

In the days when orders had to be placed by telephone and relied on several steps between investor and exchange floor, it was impossible to have heavy volume days when indices would move many points. This was true simply because the systems could not handle heavy trade volume; so on those days when high volume of orders were being placed, the delays spilled over to after-hours and the following trading day. The resources simply were not available.

Up until 1972, the DJIA had not moved above 1,000. By the end of 1990 the DJIA was around 2,600, and in 1995 the index went above 5,000 for the first time. Most of the upward movement in the years since occurred *after* Internet access to markets became available. This does not mean the Internet was solely responsible for movement of the index. But it does mean that the Internet made it much easier for big point movement to occur, where it could not have done so before.

In the past, one-day price movement in the double digits was considered significant, but today triple-digit change is not at all unusual. In the future, triple-movement days will very likely be more the norm than the exception. However, this does not mean that the markets today are more volatile than in the past. During the 1980s, when the market was between 1,000 and 2,000, movement of 15 to 20 points was a big day. But 20 points relative to a DJIA at 1,500 is a 1.3 percent move. When the Dow is at 13,000, a 1.3 percent change equals about 170 points.

With Internet access, millions of individual investors get trades executed right on the exchange floor, making it cheaper and faster than ever before, which opens up a range of new markets beyond long-position stocks. These include short-position stocks, long and short trades in options and futures, REITs, exchange-traded funds, mortgage-backed securities, and many other products that were not even conceived of 20 years ago. In some respects, greater access has made the stock market more volatile than ever before, but cheaper, faster access has also made the market more efficient. In times of high volatility, a greater number of individual investors have opportunities to trade price swings that often move 200 points or more in a matter of an hour or less. Only a few decades ago, when the market was under 1,000, such wide point swings were simply unimaginable.

Given ever-faster systems and improved communications speed it is likely that in the future, even bigger point spreads will occur in the markets. What used to be a fairly cumbersome trading system is so efficient today that the markets have had to employ programmed trading curbs simply to prevent runaway prices in either direction.

Trading in a specific stock is halted, for example, if news of a merger or other major event will likely affect price. Restrictions are lifted and trading allowed to resume once the news dies down, or is confirmed. Market-wide trading curbs (also called circuit breakers) are put in place whenever indices move a predetermined number of points or change by a specified percentage, either upward or downward within a single time frame (such as a trading day or number of hours). With these curbs, large point changes seen during times of market panics are prevented in a single day. Within the space between trading days the panic is likely to cool off, allowing markets to maintain some equilibrium and a more sensible and orderly level of change from day to day.

Online Investing: Practical, Cheap, and Accessible

The amazing changes in access to the market—speed, accessibility, and information—have created a revolution. It is important to realize that until the late nineteenth century, the ordinary citizen did not have access to the stock exchange in any manner. Only brokers could make trades. The only way for people to put money into stocks was to befriend a broker. There was no public exchange access. In fact, there were no telephones or computers either. A series of key inventions have revolutionized investing over the past 150 years. These include the telegraph, telephone, computer, and the Internet.

All of these inventions were obvious advantages, but only in hindsight. At the time, resistance to change was strong and it took an entire generation to overcome older ways of thinking. An illustration of this occurred as this book was nearing completion:

> I met with a friend from the days when I worked in a small securities firm. She is a professional planner with many years' experience, and is probably the most knowledgeable businessperson I know. She is in her mid-60s, meaning she was not raised using computers.
>
> The discussion turned to investing and she commented that her stock market activity was not as much as she would like, because she was concerned about paying $30 per trade to her broker. The firm she mentioned was the same one I use and I pay only $10 per online trade.
>
> I asked why she was paying $30, and she said she always made trades by phone. The reason was twofold: First, she did not trust computers. Second, she wants to deal with a real person directly so that if her trade was ill-advised, that person could tell her so.

Remember, this is an experienced and intelligent person. But our discussion is quite revealing. An entire generation of people, often the most active investors, were not raised with the Internet and there remains a trust issue that most younger investors do not suffer from. But more revealing was the reliance on person-to-person contact. The truth is, the order-placement person on a discount broker's phone line is not an adviser, and is unlikely to question a client's trade decisions. Even so, this exceptionally experienced investor was unable to accept the speed, convenience, economy, and obvious benefits of the computer and the Internet. The need for old-style contact was more powerful.[3]

The lesson to be learned from this is that change, especially major change, can be invariably hard to accept. When the telephone was first introduced, most people insisted they would never place one in their homes. "Why," they asked, "would a person want to put a box in their homes allowing anyone to summon them at all hours or during meals?"

Similar resistance applied to the invention of the typewriter. The first such machine, the Sholes & Glidden Type Writer, was manufactured by Remington in the 1870s, and hoping to get publicity for the new technology, one of the first models was sent to Mark Twain. He tried to get accustomed to it, but did not take to it right away. Later, he was the first author to submit a book manuscript in type (*Life on the Mississippi*, 1883). But even then, he did not type it up himself. The book was a typed copy of his handwritten manuscript. For most people, the new technology was simply too complicated. Twain wrote about his experience:

> Please do not even divulge the fact that I own a machine. I have entirely stopped using the Type-Writer, for the reason that I never could write a letter with it to anybody without receiving a request by return mail that I would not only describe the machine but state what progress I had made in the use of it, etc., etc. I don't like to write letters, and so I don't want people to know that I own this curiosity-breeding little joker.[4]

Writers also resisted the advent of word processing in the 1980s. Some believed that using a computer would take away from their typewriter-focused creativity, or somehow that the computer would replace their art. This belief quickly vanished, however, when the automated cut-and-paste feature made endless retyped drafts obsolete.

Even today, many investors suffer from the same resistance to computerization of trading transactions, and the Internet is viewed suspiciously. This is understandable among older people, who were raised without the Internet and lack computers in any form. Today this age group represents a disproportionate segment of the individual investing world, because those in baby-boomer ages and up are a large part of the U.S. population. However, the obvious advantages of automation will eventually dominate the investing world. The fact that efficiency makes it possible to experience triple-digit trading days makes the point well. In the "old days," hand-placed orders communicated by telephone limited the potential volume of trades in the few hours the market is open. Today, no one even blinks at record-level volume, and no one pauses to ask how the exchange and brokerage systems can handle that volume. It is taken for granted that automated systems are lightning fast, and trade execution occurs in most cases within seconds of the order being placed.

▓ Unexpected Losses and Planned Profits

Of course, there is a downside to super-fast order placement in the stock market. If mistakes are made, they are made very quickly in today's speed-of-light technological world. Few people speak directly to a broker about their trade decisions, so there are no opportunities for someone to warn you about errors. However, in reality, the old system was no better than today's. Stockbrokers were never known to give good advice to clients. In fact, they were more likely to telephone clients and push specific stocks (invariably those the firm was underwriting itself), whether they were sound investments or not. The track record of stockbrokers and advisers was dismal. Widely publicized abuses by big Wall Street firms like Merrill Lynch resulted in billion-dollar fines. In fact, the whole system of advisory services was so poor that the value of relying on someone was highly questionable.

The "experts" continued recommending Enron stock even after the company's problems began to emerge. Overall, traditional firms issued overwhelming "buy" recommendations with only a few "hold" and virtually no "sell" recommendations to their clients. The advice was often the result of glaring conflicts of interest, with the investment advisory services coming from the same company underwriting large blocks of stock for client companies. The result was extremely poor advice to clients, and millions of dollars were lost between 2000 and 2002 as a consequence.

Today, many wise investors have confronted a reality: *When it comes to managing your money wisely, you are on your own.* It would be nice if there were experts out there who could provide you with the kind of advice you would like and often need. But even that minority of exceptionally honest and talented brokers and financial planners, who know what they are taking about, cannot be expected to care for your money as well as you will.

When you experience losses in stock positions, which you have to expect in some number of trades, you can write them off to the odds. But if you are taken by surprise, this is a sign that you did not prepare yourself well enough. Even for those relying on advice from other people, losses are a surprise. But when you do your own homework, losses can be viewed as part of the game. The key, however, is to create a system of analysis that reduces the rate of losses so that you can beat the averages. Thus, losses will not have to be seen as surprises. The overall profits will be the result of a well-executed plan.

Everyone deserves a fair chance at building wealth. This occurs through a program of budgeting and savings, an understanding of your own risk tolerance, and building a portfolio that is a good match for you. It also involves owning your home and carrying the appropriate kinds of insurance that everyone needs: life, health, homeowners, and other essential protection. But in the stock market, you cannot get a guarantee for the safety of your money. There are no guarantees. Because you are on your own, you have to pick investments with great care; risks cannot be avoided, but they can be managed well. As you build your wealth over time, the combination of your family home and a growing portfolio of exceptional stocks will build the security and safety everyone wants and deserves.

▓ Notes

1 *Sources:* Department of Health and Human Services, National Center for Health Statistics; *National Vital Statistics Reports,* vol. 54, no. 19, June 28, 2006. Web site: *www.dhhs.gov.*
2 Source: Eastman Kodak 2006 annual report.
3 Author's discussion with a friend shortly before completion of this book.
4 Mark Twain, Letter, March 19, 1875.

GLOSSARY

acid test alternate name for the quick assets ratio, which is current ratio excluding inventory.

annual report a report issued by publicly held corporations, including financial statements and footnotes; management discussion; and additional disclosure and promotional sections.

annualized return the return on investment calculated on a full-year basis, meaning increasing the rate if held less than one year, or reducing the rate if held for more than one year. To calculate, divide return by the holding period (in months, and multiply the result by 12 months).

asset allocation a form of diversification, in which emphasis is placed on dividing capital among separate markets (stocks, bonds, real estate, money markets).

back-end sales load a type of charge assessed by a mutual fund at a future date rather than at the time funds are invested.

balance sheet a report issued by a corporation as of a fixed date, usually the end of a quarter or fiscal year, in which the ending balances are reported for all asset, liability, and shareholders' equity accounts.

balanced fund a mutual fund including both equity and debt in its portfolio.

breakaway gap a type of gap in trading in which the price range moves above or below the previously established trading range, including a space between a previous day's closing price and the current day's opening price.

break-even return a calculation of the return required to break even after
allowing for both inflation and taxes.

breakout a movement of price of a stock above or below an established
trading range.

call a type of option granting its owner the right, but not the obligation,
to buy 100 shares of a specified stock, at a fixed price and on or
before a specified expiration date in the future.

capital gains or losses investment gains or losses; short-term refers to
holding periods of one year or less, and long-term capital gains or
losses (with a favorable tax rate) refers to holding periods beyond
one full year.

capital value-weighted index a market index in which companies with
greater dollar value of capital hold greater weight within the index.

closed-end fund a type of mutual fund that does not accept funds from
new investors.

common gap a trading gap, or space between one day's close and the
next day's opening price, which occurs periodically and not necessarily as part of a change in the trading range or trend.

compound return the return on investment including reinvested dividends used to purchase additional partial shares, so that each quarter's dividend return is based on a greater overall base.

congestion a trading pattern in which price action pauses or moves sideways.

Consumer Price Index (CPI) statistic published by the Bureau of Labor
Statistics, combining many economic trends; most often used as the
definitive level of inflation.

contrarian investing a strategy involving making decisions contrary to
the prevalent opinion, due to an observation that in the market, the
majority is wrong more often than right.

core earnings developed by Standard & Poor's, an adjustment to reported earnings to reflect only the revenues, costs, and expenses of the
corporation's primary business, and excluding nonrecurring items.

covered call a type of call sold by an investor who owns 100 shares of
stock; in the event the call is exercised, the investor has the shares to
deliver, so that risk is lower than that with an uncovered call.

current assets and liabilities those assets convertible to cash within one
year, and liabilities due and payable within one year.

current ratio a calculation of working capital, in which the total of all current assets is divided by all current liabilities; the resulting ratio is reported as a single digit.

current yield the yield from dividends on a stock investment, which changes each time the market value of stock rises or falls.

day trading activity involving moving in and out of positions within a single trading day.

debt capitalization a form of capitalization from borrowings, most commonly reported as long-term notes or corporate bonds.

debt ratio the percentage of long-term debt to total capitalization (long-term debt plus stockholders' equity).

distribution fee (12b-1) a fee charged by many mutual funds to pay for the cost of advertising, allowed under SEC rule 12b-1.

diversification investing capital in enough different stocks, sectors, or markets to avoid large losses from any single event, such as a decline in price following a negative earnings surprise, poor economic news, or consumer buying trends.

dividend yield also called current yield, the amount of dividends divided by the market value of stock.

dollar-cost averaging a technique in which investors place the same amount of capital into the market periodically, regardless of whether prices rise or fall.

Dow Theory a technical theory used to predict long-term market sentiment and trends (bull or bear markets), first described by S.A. Nelson in his book, *The ABC of Stock Speculation*, and based on the writings of Charles Dow.

earnings per share (EPS) the total earnings of a company (usually per quarter or per fiscal year), divided by the number of outstanding shares, and expressed in a dollar-and-cent value.

effective tax rate the rate individuals pay based on taxable income (total income minus adjustments, exclusions, and deductions), expressed as a percentage.

efficient market hypothesis a theory stating that all crucial information about a company and its stock is known by the market at large, and reflected in the current price at all times.

enterprise value the estimated value of a company if it were to be liquidated, and not considering any value for future growth or profits; current tangible assets minus liabilities.

equity capitalization the total of capitalization raised from the sale of stock, adjusted upward or downward by retained earnings, dividends declared and paid, and other equity adjustments; distinguished from debt capitalization, which is raised from issuing bonds and other long-term debt obligations.

equity fund a type of mutual fund focusing on stock ownership, and excluding bonds and other debt holdings.

exchange fee a fee charged to move mutual fund investments within a family of funds.

exchange-traded fund (ETF) a type of mutual fund with a preidentified basket of stocks, traded on the public exchanges instead of through the fund's management.

exercise the act of buying stock at a fixed price through ownership of a call (calling away stock), or selling stock at a fixed price through ownership of a put (putting stock to the seller).

exhaustion gap a type of gap (between a previous closing price and current opening price) occurring at the end of a price run, signaling a change in price direction.

expiration date the date when an option becomes worthless, following the third Friday of the expiration month.

fixed income fund a type of mutual fund focusing on bonds, in which income is contractually promised by the issuing agency or company.

footnotes a section of the annual report expanding on reported financial results, disclosing items not shown on the financial statements (such as contingent liabilities), or discussing risks of business activity; usually the longest section of the annual report.

front-end sales load the most common type of load mutual fund, in which the sales fee is deducted from invested capital at the time it is deposited with the fund.

fundamental analysis the analysis of a company concentrating on its capital strength and earnings, especially established trends, compared with technical analysis, which focuses mostly on a stock's price trends.

fundamental volatility the degree of consistency and predictability from year to year in reported revenues and earnings; low fundamental volatility is more desirable for most investors because it is easier to calculate likely future trend entries.

gap any trading pattern in which space is seen between the trading range in one day and the trading range of the next day, either above or below.

global fund a mutual fund investing its portfolio in many markets outside of the United States.

growth fund a mutual fund emphasizing a portfolio believed to offer the best chance for growth in the market value of its stocks.

head and shoulders a pattern in technical analysis in which three price increases occur, with the middle level (the head) higher than the first and third levels (shoulders), believed to anticipate coming price movement downward and away from those tops.

income fund a mutual fund investing in income-producing stocks (via dividends) and debt instruments (via bonds and money market instruments).

income statement a financial report summarizing revenues, costs, expenses, and profits during a specified period of time, usually a quarter or full fiscal year.

index fund a mutual fund based on the components on an index such as the Dow Jones Industrial Average or the S&P 500.

inflation risk the risk of loss in purchasing power resulting from inflation; if an investment's yield is lower than the rate of inflation, it creates such a loss.

large-cap fund a mutual fund investing in larger companies, measured by the total dollar value of its capital.

leverage the use of money to control a greater dollar value of investments, achieved through borrowed money (on margin, for example) or through the use of options.

liquidity risk (a) the risk that the value in a portfolio will be fully invested, so that no funds are available for further purchases; (b) in terms of a company's working capital, the risk that available funds will not be sufficient to continue paying current liabilities or to expand operations.

load fund a mutual fund that charges a sales commission to investors.

long-term assets a company's investment in real estate, autos and trucks, tools, machinery, furniture, and other assets that are depreciated over a specified recovery period.

long-term liabilities any liabilities payable beyond the next 12 months as of the date of the balance sheet.

lost opportunity risk the risk that newly discovered and potentially profitable investments cannot be made because available funds are fully invested.

market risk the best-known form of risk that a stock's value will fall rather than rise.

mid-cap fund a mutual fund seeking investments in mid-size companies, believed to offer the most advantageous growth potential.

money market fund a mutual fund with portfolio holdings in money market instruments only (certificates of deposit, treasury obligations, short-term notes, bankers acceptances, and other instruments).

mortgage pool an investment similar to a mutual fund, but holding mortgages rather than stocks or bonds.

mutual fund an organization that combines the capital of many investors to purchase a diversified portfolio of stocks, bonds, or a combination of both.

net asset value (NAV) the current market value of a mutual fund, representing the total of assets minus liabilities, and divided by the number of outstanding shares.

net profit the "bottom line" of the income statement, including operating profit adjusted for nonoperating income and expenses and for tax liabilities.

net return the percentage of net profit, divided by total revenues.

no-load fund a mutual fund that does not charge investors a sales commission.

nondiversification risk the risk of investing in too narrow a portfolio, meaning that a single event in a company, sector, or the economy may affect the entire portfolio in a negative manner.

open-end fund any mutual fund that will accept new investors, compared with a closed-end fund that excludes additional participation.

operating profit the profit from operations, before adjusting for nonoperating items (capital gains, currency exchange gains or losses, interest income or expense, etc.) or for tax liabilities.

options intangible instruments with a limited life span, allowing traders to speculate on price movement in stocks; a call provides its owner with the right to buy 100 shares at a fixed price, and a put provides its owner with the right to sell 100 shares at a fixed price.

overdiversification risk the risk that a portfolio is so diversified that overall net returns will approximate rather than beat the market.

pattern day trader any trader who moves in and out of the same position in the market four or more times within five consecutive trading days; under the SEC rules for pattern day trading, this level of activity can be undertaken only when $25,000 or more is left on deposit with the brokerage firm in the form of cash or securities.

Ponzi scheme a con game in which high returns are promised, and old investors are paid from funds raised from new investors. These schemes eventually crash, causing large losses; named after the infamous Charles Ponzi who promised investors they would double their money in 90 days, active during the 1920s.

premium the current value of an option contract.

price-to-earnings (P/E) ratio the current market price per share of stock, divided by the company's earnings per share in the latest reported quarter or fiscal year.

price-weighted index any market index in which the more expensive stocks have greater weight, the best-known of which is the Dow Jones Industrial Average.

pro forma "as a matter of form," any financial report that estimates actual outcome, often associated with reporting of income from pension fund assets.

pump and dump an illiquid act in which investors buy shares of stock, promote the stock on investment chat lines to create interest and more demand (pump), and then sell their shares at inflated value (dump).

put an option granting its owner the right, but not the obligation, to sell 100 shares of a specified stock at a fixed price on or before a specified expiration date.

quick assets ratio the current ratio, excluding the value of inventory; also called the acid test.

random walk theory a theory stating that all market price movement is random, and that the chances of a stock's price rising or falling is 50–50.

real estate investment trust (REIT) a conduit investment that trades on public exchanges; the REIT invests in property (equity REIT) or lends money (mortgage REIT) or may combine both activities (hybrid REIT).

redemption fee a fee charged by a mutual fund to investors when shares are sold.

Regulation SHO an SEC regulation restricting short sales (SHO), especially uncovered, or naked short sales.

reinvested dividends action when dividends are applied to purchase additional partial shares rather than taken in cash; this creates a compound rate of return on dividend yield.

resistance the top level of an existing trading range, above which prices are not expected to rise until a breakout occurs; the opposite of support.

retained earnings the net sum total of profits or losses from operations each year, and part of stockholders' equity.

reverse head and shoulders a head and shoulders pattern occurring on the bottom of the trading range and testing support, believed to anticipate a subsequent rise in price levels.

risk tolerance an individual's ability to accept a known and defined level of market risk and other forms of risk in the stock market.

runaway gap a trading gap that continues in one direction over several trading days.

sales load a commission charged by a mutual fund.

small-cap fund a mutual fund emphasizing small corporations in their portfolios, as measured by capital value.

specialty fund any mutual fund defined by its emphasis on a specific market sector, country, commodity, or industry.

stockholders' equity the net worth of a corporation, consisting of all classes of stock, retained earnings, and adjustments for dividends declared and other additions to or reductions from equity.

striking price the fixed price at which options can be exercised, regardless of movement in the current market price of the stock.

support the bottom level of a trading range, the price below which prices are not expected to extend until the current range is violated with a breakout; the opposite of resistance.

swing trading a technique involving moving in and out of long or short positions in three- to five-day cycles or short-term trends.

tax risk the risk that marginal profits will be reduced by federal and state tax liabilities; or that long-term capital gains will be lost when positions are closed before one full year.

tax-free bond fund a mutual fund specializing in a portfolio of municipal bonds and other tax-free debt instruments.

technical analysis any form of analysis focused on price and volume action rather than on a company's financial results.

total capitalization the sum of all debt capitalization (bonds and long-term notes) and equity capitalization (stockholders' equity).

trading range the space between resistance and support, the range of prices at which stocks trade.

uncovered call a call written without also owning 100 shares of stock, considered high risk because losses are in theory unlimited; in comparison, a covered call is a very conservative strategy.

value fund a mutual fund emphasizing high-quality companies whose stock is expected to outperform the market over the long term.

volatility the tendency for prices to move in a specified price range; the most popular format for defining market risk.

weighted average an average in which later entries are given greater weight than earlier entries in the field, on the theory that more recent activity is more relevant to the trend.

INDEX